CHESS
for Children

Author Ted Nottingham with national champion school chess club in South Lincolnshire, England.

CHESS
for Children

Ted Nottingham,
BobWade &
Al Lawrence

Sterling Publishing Co., Inc.   New York

Edited by Claire Bazinet

Library of Congress Cataloging-in-Publication Data

Nottingham, Ted.
Chess for children / Ted Nottingham, Bob Wade & Al Lawrence.
p.   cm.
Includes index.
Summary: Uses the revolutionary Lincolnshire system to explain how
to play, enjoy, and master chess and recounts anecdotes about
notable players in the history of the game.
ISBN 0-8069-0452-6
1. Chess—Juvenile literature. [1. Chess.] I. Wade, Robert
Graham. II. Lawrence, Al. III. Title.
GV1446.N66 1993
794.1—dc20   93-24832
                                                         CIP
                                                          AC

1 3 5 7 9 8 6 4 2

Published in 1993 by Sterling Publishing Company, Inc.
387 Park Avenue South, New York, N.Y. 10016
© 1993 by Ted Nottingham, Bob Wade and Al Lawrence
Distributed in Canada by Sterling Publishing
% Canadian Manda Group, P.O. Box 920, Station U
Toronto, Ontario, Canada M8Z 5P9
Distributed in Great Britain and Europe by Cassell PLC
Villiers House, 41/47 Strand, London WC2N 5JE, England
Distributed in Australia by Capricorn Link Ltd.
P.O. Box 665, Lane Cove, NSW 2066
Manufactured in the United States of America
All rights reserved

Sterling ISBN 0-8069-0452-6

To a great and lovely friend,
the late Michael Hogarth of Birgham, Scotland

ACKNOWLEDGMENTS

Thanks and acknowledgments are offered to:

Charles G. Nurnberg, a patient and
understanding publisher

Claire Bazinet, a most thoughtful and thorough editor

Elliott Winslow of the U.S. Chess Federation
for doing the diagrams

Geoff Brown and Andrew Oglesby for taking and preparing
the photographs

Gerald Baxter for the loan of his board and chessmen

Gerald's daughter and her husband, Jane and Tony Ball, for
their children, David and Sarah, as models

Hilary Armstrong for typing the manuscript and needed
correspondence and Jenny van Gemeren for
typing some faxes

Jean Driver, M.A., Koby Fairbanks, and Gillian Nottingham
for their proofreading help

Nigel Hancock and the staff of First Choice Cabs and
Couriers for the use of their fax machine and their kind
interest in the project

The late Tom Driberg, M.P., for "An International Language,"
from his report in *The Reynolds News*, London, 1947

Sybil Marshall, M.A., author of *A Nest of Magpies*,
for her introductory poem, "The Game of Kings"

The late Phyllis Woodall for "The Pawn's Story"

Lincolnshire teacher Allan R. Lewis, ex-chairman of
Spalding Chess Club, for "The Starship Knight"

And to my brother, Gordon Nottingham, who first suggested
the idea of this book

CONTENTS

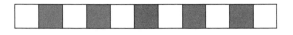

U.S. Chess Federation, New Windsor, NY

U.S. Chess Federation, New Windsor, NY

PART ONE

INTRODUCING CHESS

An International Language

It was early in 1945. Just as the Western Allies were pouring through France on their way to Germany, so the Soviet Red Army was making a big push against the German divisions massed along the Eastern front. In Budapest, the capital city of Hungary, hand-to-hand fighting raged as the Germans fought fiercely over every inch of territory. Yet, below ground, in an air-raid shelter, a fourteen-year-old Hungarian boy sat quietly playing chess with a German soldier, both for the moment safe from the noise and fighting outside. Suddenly another German called in a warning. Red Army soldiers were in the street! The Germans had to leave immediately.

A few minutes later, a Soviet soldier burst into the cellar, waving his submachine gun around. Someone screamed. Then the soldier saw the unfinished chess game and the Hungarian boy sitting before it. Realizing that he was in no danger, the Soviet soldier, only a young man himself, lowered his gun. He sat down on the other side of the board and won the game that the German—his enemy—had started. After the war, the young Hungarian said that those two soldiers, the German and the Soviet, were two of the nicest people he had ever met!

The moral of this story is clear. Chess is an international game, a world game, crossing all boundaries, even those of war. Even those who cannot speak each other's language can play together. After you have read this book, you will be able to play chess with anybody, young or old, of any nationality.

♟ ♟ DID YOU KNOW? ♟ ♟

In perhaps the greatest film of all time, *Casablanca*, Humphrey Bogart played chess in Rick's café. It was only natural since Bogart, one of cinema's great stars, was himself a chess addict.

How Chess Began

A young English headmaster, Harold James Murray, who a hundred years ago taught himself Arabic and read the first early manuscripts on chess, is credited with finding out how chess started. The account he wrote was published in 1913 as *A History*

Author Ted Nottingham with some of the children from the South Lincolnshire school chess club.

of Chess. Murray discovered that the first great players were Arabs and their "aliyats" were the first grandmasters. In fact, the first world champion could be considered to be an Arab named Al-Suli. Haroun al-Rashid, Caliph of Baghdad, said that the roses in the palace garden were wonderful, but Al-Suli's chess was even better. These Arabs of over one thousand years ago were real chess fans. Even one of the one-thousand-and-one stories told by the slave girl Scheherazade to the Caliph Haroun in *The Arabian Nights*, was about chess.

The game spread. Travelling chess sets were invented by the Vikings so that they could play during rough seas as they voyaged in their longships. The chess boards had little holes punched in them and the chessmen had small pegs in their bases to fit into the holes.

When West met East with the Crusaders battling to recapture Jerusalem, it's possible that real-life opponents faced off over the chessboard. Saladin is even said to have taught Richard the Lionheart how to play.

It was during this time that the rules changed. The changes were only small, but they greatly speeded up the game. The pawn was now allowed to go two squares on its first move and the bishop was free to go as many squares diagonally as it liked. Most importantly, instead of moving diagonally one square at a time, the new queen could go as many squares as she liked *in any direction*. This new go-everywhere queen could now deliver checkmate in four moves!

When the Crusaders went home they took chess with them and today the game is played all over the world. This book will introduce you to this game, truly the "game of kings."

The Great Learn Young

You're never too old to begin playing chess. You're never too young, either. The young American Paul Morphy learned to play at home in New Orleans by watching his father and uncle play. In 1858, at the age of twenty-one, Paul visited Europe and convincingly beat the best players in the world.

See this list of world champions:

Wilhelm Steinitz reigned as world champion from 1866 to 1894. He learned to play at the age of twelve.

Emanuel Lasker was ten years old when taught to play by his older brother Berthold. Emanuel was world champion from 1894 to 1921.

José Raúl Capablanca, born in 1888, was the best four-year-old chess player of all time. He quietly picked up the moves by watching his father playing with a friend. One day his father moved a knight not according to the rules and won. Young José amazed everyone by pointing out the error. His father was very embarrassed. He challenged the boy to

a game: the four-year-old won. A few days later José's father took the little boy to his local chess club. By the age of twelve, Capablanca was the leading Cuban master. He was world champion from 1921 to 1927.

J.R. Capablanca.

Alexander Alekhine was not yet twelve when he started to play. As a boy he played many games by letter. He was world champion from 1927 to 1935 and from 1937 to 1945.

Max Euwe was taught by his mother when he was four. He won his first tournament at ten.

Mikhail Botvinnik learned to play at the age of twelve. The next year he won his school championship. He was world champion from 1948 to 1957, 1958 to 1960, and also from 1961 to 1963.

Vassily Smyslov had a good grasp of the game by the time he was six and a half. He was world champion from 1957 to 1958. In 1984, at the age of sixty-two, he reached the final four of the world championship elimination cycle.

Tigran Petrosian was not yet nine when he learned the moves by watching the play at the officers' club where his father was a caretaker. Tigran was world champion from 1963 to 1969.

Bobby Fischer was taught by his sister when he was six. He became United States champion when he was fourteen and an international grandmaster at fifteen. He won the world title in 1972, but failed to agree to conditions for defending it in 1975.

Mikhail Tal watched his father's medical patients playing in the waiting room. By the age of ten he had won at school a diploma for chess. He was champion from 1960 to 1961.

Boris Spassky was world champion from 1969 to 1972. He learned to play when he was five, as an evacuee from the besieged city of Leningrad.

Anatoly Karpov became world champion in 1975. Like Capablanca he learned to play at the age of four. Although he lived in an isolated, mountainous part of Russia he made steady progress. He was Russian master at fifteen, international grandmaster at nineteen, and world champion at twenty-three.

Gary Kasparov, current world champion since 1985, learned to play at the age of six.

The Game of Kings

Ever since the world began
Man has been at war with man,
Kings and queens set up the fights
Called in bishops, sent for knights;
Rooked castles from each other, then
Captured and killed each other's men.

So it went on, till one side said
"Hurrah! We've won! Their king is dead!"
But when there were no wars to fight
They all grew bored, as well they might.
They fought each other just the same
Except twas turned into a game.

Played on a board with little men
We've played their game—called chess—since then.
Each contest now is just as keen
As theirs on battlefield had been;
In cunning moves the war's still fought
By complex rules exactly taught.

Our "game of kings" is skilled and clever
But no one's slain, or wounded ever.
Black tackles White with brains, not brawn
As queen, rook, bishop, knight and pawn
Are banished from the chequered deck
And either Black or White calls "Check!"

Or, as the ancient Persians said,
"Shah mat! Your king is dead!"

Sybil Marshall

Left to right, Sophia, Judith, and Susan Polgar.

The Polgar Sisters

Daughters of the game.
Shakespeare—*Troilus and Cressida*

The Polgar sisters are chess's new sensations. The oldest sister Susan, just in her twenties, has the grandmaster title. The youngest, Judith, is just sixteen. She reached the grandmaster title at the age of fifteen, younger than even the celebrated Bobby Fischer was when he made grandmaster. Judith is now in the world's top forty and has just earned $120,000 by beating ex–world champion Boris Spassky in a match. They are to chess perhaps what the Brontë sisters were to literature. Whereas the Brontës grew up in England with the wild moors on one side

of their house in Haworth and the smoky black industry of the valleys on the other side, the Polgars grew up in a small flat in Budapest. Members of their family were killed in Adolf Hitler's concentration camps, and it is as if some demon of vengeance is in their brilliant play. Arguments still rage over which of literature's Brontë sisters had the

---

♛ ♛ **DID YOU KNOW?** ♛ ♛

In Lewis Carroll's *Through the Looking Glass*, the adventurous Alice is a pawn who meets living chess pieces in a mirror world. Alice and the story's characters actually move according to the rules of chess.

---

greatest talent and Hollywood has made films of their dark tempestuous stories. There are similar arguments over the Polgars. At the moment Judith's achievement in becoming a grandmaster at fifteen places her in the lead, but nobody is really sure. Look what happened only four years ago, in 1989.

The organizers in Rome announced an international tournament and invited, among others, five international masters and five grandmasters. Everybody knew about the strong play of Judith and Susan but nobody knew about Sofia. On paper she did not have a chance—she was nowhere in the world's top thousand best players, and she was only fourteen. This is what happened in her nine games:

With eight wins and a draw, for 8½ points out of 9, Sofia had won the tournament!

Everybody knew that Susan was excellent and Judith was brilliant but here was Sofia turning in a performance light-ears ahead of anything she had done previously and at a tender age. Maybe there was no game as brilliant in her tournament as thirteen-year-old Fischer's against Donald Byrne in the Lessing Rosenwald 1956 tournament in New York. There the seventeenth move of Fischer's Grunfeld Defense may well, as some commentators assert, "be talked about for centuries to come." But in New York, the young Fischer lost more games than he won. Here in Rome, Sofia had romped away with the tournament, beating the second-place

			SOFIA POLGAR		
Game	Opponent	Title	World Rating	Outcome	Sofia's Score
1	Rabczevsky	None	2200	Win Polgar	1/1
2	Cardinal	None	2200	Win Polgar	2/2
3	Palatnik	Grandmaster	2470	Win Polgar	3/3
4	D'Amore	International Master	2425	Win Polgar	4/4
5	Chernin	Grandmaster	2580	Win Polgar	5/5
6	Suba	Grandmaster	2515	Win Polgar	6/6
7	Mrdja	Master	2405	Win Polgar	7/7
8	Razuvayev	Grandmaster	2550	Win Polgar	8/8
9	Dolmatov	Grandmaster	2580	Draw	8½/9

finisher by a clear two points. Sofia's tournament result may well be the greatest ever produced by a fourteen-year-old, and that should be indication enough of her ability.

There is much discussion in the chess world about these three brilliant sisters. It will not be long before the whole world hears about them, and who knows but one or more of them might become world champion. The Polgars are making chess history. Watch out for them!

U.S. Chess Federation, New Windsor, NY

. . . while sister Sophia plays a young boy.

U.S. Chess Federation, New Windsor, NY

Judith and Susan Polgar play grandmaster Pal Benko at 1992 Chessathon in New York . . .

♜ ♖ **DID YOU KNOW?** ♖ ♜

Chess is played in nearly every country in the world. It offers never-ending variety. After only two moves each, more than 70,000 different moves are possible. No two games are ever alike, although an end-game from a manuscript by Al-Adli from the ninth century cropped up in an actual game in Denmark in 1945.

Photo by Robert Rathbone, Nottingham, UK

Enjoying Chess

The one aim in chess is to checkmate or capture the opponent's king. To enjoy chess you will need to know how your pieces can attack and capture and you will need to move your pieces with effect and with power.

If you are going to play well, you must learn to master these skills:

- how to take in at a glance all of the squares to which a piece can go, before you move it—or even touch it
- how to see and build up checkmating positions, even in the middle of many other pieces

- how to use such tactics as *forks* and *pins* to win your enemy's pieces
- how to figure out "What is my opponent trying to do?" so that you can either attack, defend, or counter with a new plan
- how to checkmate, and be constantly aware of all the checkmating positions

These skills are best mastered by playing chess as often as you can, but it is also important to study the great games and positions of past and present champions. Many of the games in this book are specially designed to teach you the action of each chessman. In chess the winner is nearly always the player who has the most active pieces and who uses them all as a team. You need constant practice and good opponents to make you a really good player. So get out the chessboard and pieces and set up the positions as you find them in this, your first, training book.

Getting Ready to Play

THE CHESSBOARD

Chess is played on a large square board divided into 64 smaller squares that alternate light and dark. They are called white and black squares although the squares on the board can be any two different colors.

The board must be placed so that each player has a white square in the corner next to his or her right hand. Remember, *white on right!* A row of black squares will also run diagonally up the board from left-hand corner to opposite corner. This is how you know that the board is set up correctly for play.

FILES AND RANKS

The 64 squares of the board make up 8 up-and-down columns, called *files*, and 8 side-to-side rows, called *ranks* (8 × 8 = 64). The 8 files have letter names: **a**, **b**, **c**, **d**, **e**, **f**, **g**, and **h**. The names of the 8 ranks are: **1**, **2**, **3**, **4**, **5**, **6**, **7**, and **8**.

Because white always moves first, the letters of the 8 files, **a** through **h**, begin from white's left-hand side.

The ranks, **1** through **8**, are numbered starting from white's side of the board.

Put the file letter and the rank number of a square together (the file letter always comes first) and you have named the square.

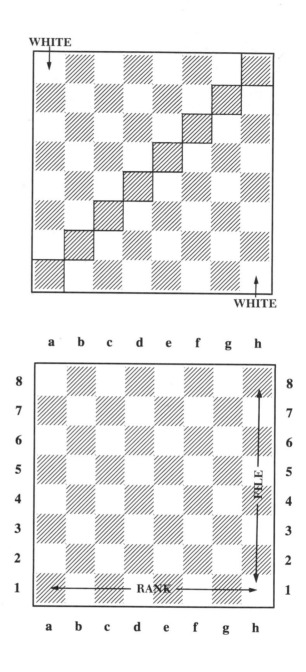

NAMING THE SQUARES

Look at the white square in the upper left-hand corner of the board here which has been marked with a star. The square is in file **a** and in rank **8**, so its name is . . . what?

If you said the starred square is **a8**, you're right! Let's try another. What square have we put a triangle in?

Place your finger on the square, then slide it up or down the file to find the square's file name. Then go back to the square and move your finger left or right to find the square's rank name. Put them both together.

That's right, the square's name is **e2**.
Now, what square is the circle in?
How about the cross?
Where is the diamond?

If you said the circle is in **c4**, the cross is in **g6**, and the diamond is in **d7**, you are right!
Wasn't that easy? Now you are well on your way to knowing algebraic notation, a system of keeping track of chess moves that is much simpler than it sounds. It is the language used by chess players all over the world.

THE PIECES AND PAWNS

Like the playing board, the chessmen that move from square to square are divided into white and black. Each player has 8 pieces: 1 king (K), 1 queen (Q), 2 bishops (B), 2 rooks (R), 2 knights (N is used because K is taken by king); and 8 pawns—a total of 16 chessmen on each side.

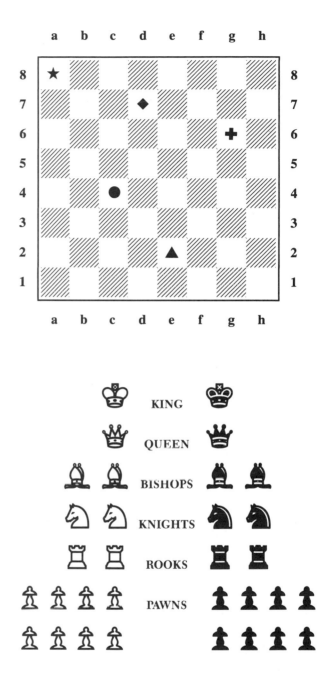

For a full game, the white pieces are placed on rank 1 with the white pawns in front of them on rank 2. The black pieces are placed on rank 8. The black pawns are in front of them on rank 7.

FOLLOWING THE MOVES

Using algebraic notation, you can follow the chessmen around the board. For example, you see **1 b2 – b4**. That tells you that, on the first move, the pawn on the **b2** square *moves to* square **b4**.

In a game, what if you see **Qd3 – h7**? Since Q stands for queen, it means that the queen moves from square **d3** to **h7**.

White always starts, moving first, then black. Five dots before a move, like . . . . . **g7 – g5**, indicate that it is black's play.

Now you can follow the moves of all the chess pieces and pawns in this book and are ready to learn to play chess. Later, you can use algebraic notation to replay other chess games that you have heard of or read about and learn from them. And, if you write down your own games in chess notation, you can play over your moves again and again and improve on them too.

You are ready to go, but first . . . one very important rule.

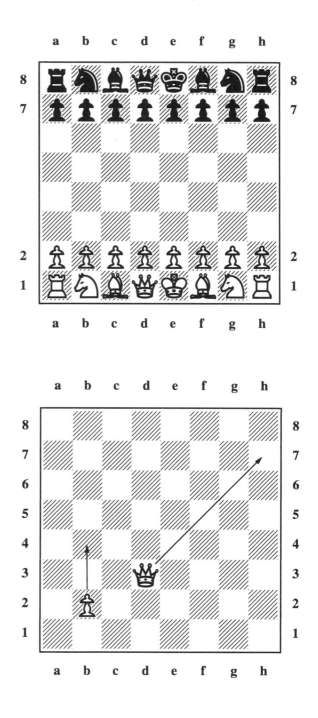

Touch and Move— Or Else!

All modern chess games are played according to the rule "If you touch a piece, you must move it." The following story, from Snorri Sturluson's *Helmskringla*, dates from the eleventh century. It shows what can happen if you do not play "touch—move."

King Canute (he was the one who once sat on a beach and commanded the waves to go back) and Ulf the Earl were playing chess. The king made a bad move and the earl took a knight from him. The king took his knight back and said he would play another move. The earl grew angry, threw down the chessboard, and stomped off.

"Are you running away, Ulf the Coward?" the king called after him. The earl answered, "You did not call me Coward when I came to your aid when the Swedes were beating you like a dog."

The angry king then ordered one of his knights to kill the earl.

When the knight returned with a bloody sword in his hand the king asked, "Have you killed the earl?"

"I have killed him," the knight said.

"You have done well," said the king.

This all happened on St. Michael's Day in the year 1027 at the then Danish capital of Roskilde. Ever since that day we have played "touch a piece, move it." We do not want any more murders associated with chess.

New York Congresswoman Nita Lowey cheers on a young player at 1992 Chessathon.

PART TWO

THE PIECES AND HOW THEY GO

THE PAWN

The fault, dear Brutus, is not in our stars,
But in ourselves, that we are underlings.
Shakespeare—*Julius Caesar*

A pawn is never called a piece. It is only a lowly pawn but it can be promoted and become a piece, even a queen! To do this, a pawn must cross the board, so pawns always move forward never backwards.

A new way to learn chess, which began in South Lincolnshire, England, is a game that uses just pawns, no pieces. The winner of this pawn game is the first to push a pawn through to the far rank. This "Lincolnshire system" is fast becoming the accepted way to teach people all over the world how to play. Even Russian chess literature now has references to the Lincolnshire system.

Now it is time for you to play the pawn game.

Top, *Sarah and David Ball start a game using only pawns.* **Below,** *David reaches the far rank for a win.*

The Pawn's Story

The pawn stood on the chessboard. It was his first time ever and he was scared. He had felt safe in the box with his fellow pawns and chess pieces. Now he didn't know what would happen.

Standing there black and shiny, he looked around. All he saw were pawns. No knights, no bishops or rooks, no kings or queens, black or white. He felt his fear recede and a powerful new feeling take its place. He was going to make a brilliant move. He was going to win the game; yes, all by himself! Boldly, he made his first move, taking *two* squares instead of one. The very next turn he moved another square.

There was a gasp of shock around him. Suddenly he was plucked from the board and thrust back into the box. The pawn lay where he had fallen, shivering with disgust at his own stupidity. With comforting eyes, the black queen took a step towards him. He turned away. He did not want to face anyone. He wanted to hide forever.

But a short time later he found himself on the board again. This time he was not so afraid, or bold, but cautious. He moved forward one square. After a couple of moves, when he felt it was time, he moved forward again. Gaining confidence, he took a white pawn, then . . . oh, no!

He had been picked up roughly and dumped unceremoniously back in the box. The pawn lay still, the pain of his failure filling him. A knight lying nearby spoke to him. "Do you really think you have any power in these games?" he said. "Don't be such a conceited fool. You're nothing unless someone moves you intelligently." The pawn was crushed. He had tried his best and where did it get him?

But before he knew it, he was standing once more on the board; a little less new, a little less shiny. A surer hand moved him forward two squares, then at a slant to take a white pawn, then forward again. It was like a country dance. As other pawns moved, he counted the squares ahead. He could see the far end of the board. Yes, ahead now! he thought. The hand hesitated above him. The pawn ached to go again. He was sure it was the right move.

The pawn concentrated. The player concentrated. As if a message had been passed, the hand touched the pawn. The pawn moved forward. A moment later, to the delight of both pawn and player, the pawn reached the eighth rank. The game was won! The pawn had found an excitement that would be there forever—every time he took part in a well-fought game of chess.

The Pawn Game

BLACK

WHITE

Pawns have very simple moves. See how they move, or "go," from following this sample game.

This is the starting position for the pawn game. The different pawns are identified by the files on which they are standing. The "a" pawn means the pawn on the "a" file, the "b" pawn is the pawn on the "b" file, etc. The white pawns are lined up along the second rank. Your opponent's black pawns are along the seventh. When we begin a full game the empty squares behind the pawns will be occupied by the pieces. White will begin.

1 c2 – c4

You move your "c" pawn two squares.

Rule: A pawn, on its first move only, is allowed to move two squares.

1 ..... d7 – d6

Your opponent has moved a pawn only one square.

2 d2 – d4

You boldly push a neighboring pawn two squares.

2 ..... e7 – e5

Your opponent moves another pawn, but this time two squares forward.

Now you can see the black "e" pawn is one square *diagonally forward* from your "d" pawn. Your "d" pawn can take black's "e" pawn.

3 d4 × e5

Your "d" pawn captures the "e" pawn. "×" means takes.

Rule: *A pawn takes diagonally one square forward.*

To capture, you remove the black pawn, and put your white one in its place.

3 ..... d6 × e5

Black's "d" pawn captures your pawn on the "e" file.

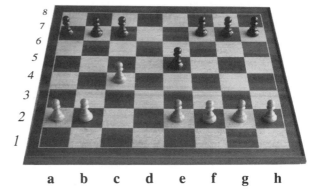

4 b2 – b4

You move your "b" pawn two squares.

4 ..... f7 – f5

Pawns only go forward. They move straight ahead unless they are capturing.

5   a2 – a4

You move your "a" pawn two squares.

5 . . . . . e5 – e4

Black's "e" pawn moves again, but now it can only go one square.

Rule: After its first move, each pawn can be played only one square per move.

6   c4 – c5

Your "c" pawn is marching on. Remember, the player whose pawn first reaches the far side of the board wins the game.

6 ..... f5 – f4

Black's "f" pawn moves forward.

7 b4 – b5

Your "b" pawn goes on.

7 ..... g7 – g5

Black has advanced his "g" pawn two squares.

8   a4 – a5

Your "a" pawn is pushed on. The big clash is just ahead.

8 ..... e4 – e3

His "e" pawn has moved again. It could take one of your pawns.

9   f2 × e3

You take first with your "f" pawn.

9 ..... f4 × e3

Your opponent recaptures with the black "f" pawn. The new "e" pawns now block each other and cannot move.

You think.

The first pawn home wins. But how can any of your three advanced pawns find a way past black's three?

10 b5 – b6

You thrust your central "b" pawn forward. You would like to take either black's "a" pawn or "c" pawn. They also can take.

10 ..... c7 × b6

Your opponent has chosen to take with the "c" pawn.

You think hard.

Your "c" pawn could be played straight ahead. It has only three squares to go. Careful! If you immediately advance it, black's **b7** pawn could gobble it. You wish that black pawn was somewhere else. How do you clear the way for your "c" pawn to go through?

11 a5 – a6

You confidently advance your "a" pawn. It is two squares—**b7** and **b8**—away from victory.

11 . . . . . b7 × a6

Your opponent takes it. Black must, or you will take on the next move.

12 c5 – c6

Your wish is granted. Black's **b7** pawn has gone. Now your "c" pawn has a clear path. Advance.

12 ..... b6 – b5

Black rushes forward the passed "b" pawn. But it will not be quick enough.

13 c6 – c7

13 ..... b5 – b4

Your "c" pawn reaches the seventh rank. It has one to go! The black "b" pawn moves again.

14 c7 – c8

You push your "c" pawn home. You've won.

In a normal game of chess, using all the pieces, this pawn is now exchanged for a white piece, usually a queen.

Note: Each side can have more than one queen.

♛ THE ♛
QUEEN

I go, I go; look how I go,
Swifter than arrow from the Tartar's bow.
   Shakespeare—*A Midsummer Night's Dream*

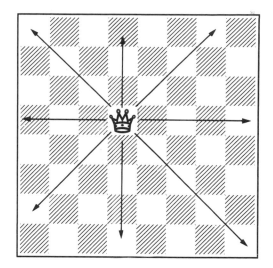

In modern chess the queen is the fastest piece on the board. This was not always so, for back in the Middle Ages she could only move one square diagonally at a time. The French of the thirteenth century called this new queen "the mad queen."

She can move in any straight line: up or down, diagonally, or side to side, as far as she likes. One square or two if need be. But no jumping! To take, she lands on a piece.

She is worth almost twice as much as any other piece on the board, except the king. World champion Capablanca once wanted to introduce a new piece he called an "ambassador," which would move like a queen and jump like a knight. The idea was not well received. Chess's queen is powerful enough. It is like the Starship *Enterprise* against World War II aircraft.

Napoleon once told his soldiers that each of them carried a Field Marshal's baton in his knapsack. So every pawn can become a queen by crossing the board.

Bobby Fischer and Tigran Petrosian once played a game with four queens on the board. It was some game. The board here shows what it looked like.

Fischer had the white pieces. Only sixteen at the time, he was playing one of the greatest grandmasters of the age. In fact, Tigran Petrosian was, in a few years, to be world champion himself. But remember, one extra queen is usually enough to win.

Can you find the four queens?

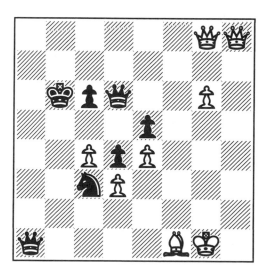

How valuable is the queen? The value of each piece in pawns is:

Knight	=	3 pawns
Bishop	=	3 pawns
Rook	=	5 pawns
Queen	=	9 pawns

So the queen's 9-pawn value is equal to one rook (5), one knight or bishop (3), and one pawn (1): $5 + 3 + 1 = 9$.

Sarah takes on David's mad queen in a Queen and Pawns Game.

The Attack of the Mad Queen

Can white handle the attack of the mad queen and get just one pawn through to the far row? That's all white needs to do to win. It's a lonely piece, but you will soon see the power of this queen as it blasts through the poorly protected pawns. The queen always starts on a square of her own color: black queen on black square **d8**, white queen on white square **d1**.

1   d2 – d3

White moves first and rescues this pawn. The queen could not now take the pawn on **d3**, because it is protected by the pawns on **c2** and **e2**. Either pawn could take the queen on the following move. The mad queen isn't that mad!

1 . . . . . Qd8 – d4

The queen leaps into battle and strikes two ways—at the pawns on **b2** and **f2**. She's not in danger from the pawn on **d3** because pawns can only capture diagonally.

2   e2 – e4

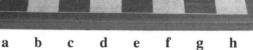

2 ..... Qd4 × b2

The queen decides to take the pawn at **b2**. White looks to see if the "e" pawn can be advanced further. No! The black queen could take it.

3 f2 – f4

White plays the "f" pawn two squares. The queen now has the choice of two pawns.

3 ..... Qb2 × c2

Do you notice the capture sign again? The queen captures to get rid of the dangerous pawns in the middle. How many pawns are now attacked?

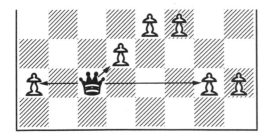

4   g2 – g4

Another pawn races forward. Three of them are only four squares away!

4   ..... Qc2 × d3

The queen captures on **d3** and chases the advanced group.

5   e4 – e5

Advance and get away from the queen! Three squares to victory.

5 ..... Qd3 – e4

6 g4 – g5

Two pawns are now only three squares
away.

6 ..... Qe4 × f4

Another × sign. Take.

7   e5 – e6

Two away!

7 ..... Qf4 × g5

The queen captures.

8   a2 – a4

Too late. Now the queen has only to mop up.

8 . . . . . Qg5 – e7

9   h2 – h4

9 . . . . . Qe7 × e6

The black queen has two plans to get rid of the last two white pawns.

She can wait along the sixth rank for the white pawns to arrive on **a6** and **h6** and then take them.

Or the queen can be played to **a6**, take the "a" pawn and then go across to the "h" file and remove the last pawn. The queen has won.

Can *you* beat the mad queen! Play a Queen and Pawns Game with you having the pawns and your opponent the queen; and then change over and see if your opponent can beat your mad queen.

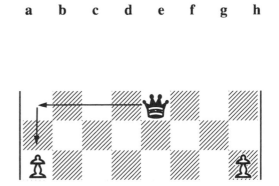

THE BISHOP

Good day to you, gentle Lord Bishop.
Shakespeare—*Henry IV, Part Two*

Look at the diagram below. The whole chessboard has sixty-four squares. Not counting the squares they are standing on, the two bishops can move, control, and attack twenty-six squares. They are a powerful team.

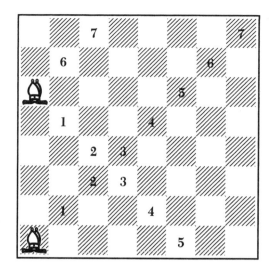

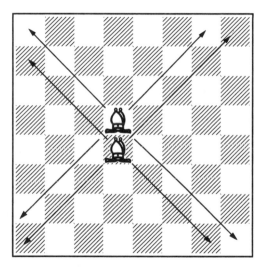

Bishops move straight along diagonals. They do not jump. They capture by landing on the square occupied by the enemy piece and then removing that piece from the board. They can take anything but a king on their landing square. Put them in the middle, where they control more squares, not on the side. The two bishops on the following board are on the side, so only control seven squares each.

Bishops

You have two bishops
One stands on black squares
Moves on black squares
Never moves on white squares.

The other stands on white squares
Never moves on black squares
Never crosses black squares
Moves only on white squares
The two never meet.

Put one in the corner
He's sleepy!
Put one at the side
He's lazy!
Put one in the center
How strong he is!

Bishops want open diagonals
Not closed ones:
Don't block their path with pawns
You know they cannot jump.

The Bishop's Test

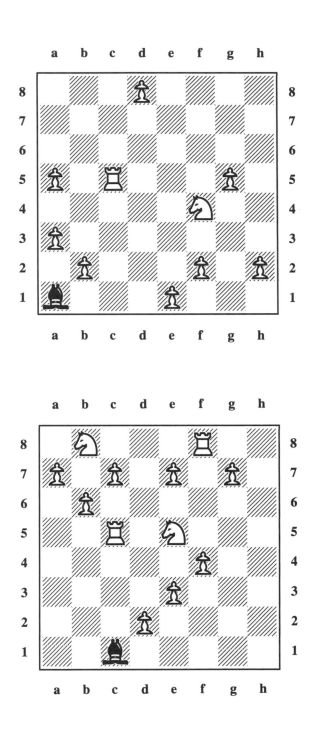

Now, how good are you with the bishop? Normally the bishop (worth only three pawns) would stand no chance. But in this game all the enemy men kindly stand still and wait for the bishop to take them off. For this test, we have ten pawns and pieces to be taken off and you only have ten moves in which to do it. Before you start, try and work out in your mind just how you are going to proceed. Can you do it?

Solution: **Ba1** × b2 × a3 × c5 × f2 × e1 × a5 × d8 × g5 × f4 × h2

NOW ANOTHER ONE

This time the bishop has to take twelve enemy men. Again, try and work it out before you begin. Remember, you must take one enemy piece or pawn with each move and you must end up by taking them all.

Solution: **Bc1** × d2 × e3 × f4 × e5 × g7 × f8 × e7 × c5 × b6 × a7 × b8 × c7

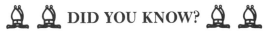 **DID YOU KNOW?**

One of the first two books to be printed in the English language, by the English printer William Caxton, was about chess. It was entitled *The Game and Play of Chess*. The other book was the Bible.

♖ THE ♖
R O O K

How many goodly creatures are there here
O brave new world, that has such people in't.
Shakespeare—*The Tempest*

Why do we call the castle a rook? We think that chess began in India and that "rukh" meant chariot in their language. Chess sets sold in Europe by the Parsee Indians pictured the rook as a small tower carried on the back of an elephant, so many people began to call it a tower or a castle.

The rook moves in straight lines, never on diagonals. Move the rook up and down the board and to the side. Feel its speed and power. Like the bishop it can only move in one direction at a time, and usually it cannot jump.

The Rook's Exercise

You have 8 moves with the white rook. The black pieces are fixed for the purposes of this game and do not move. Can you take everything on the board? Remember, you must take an enemy piece with each move.

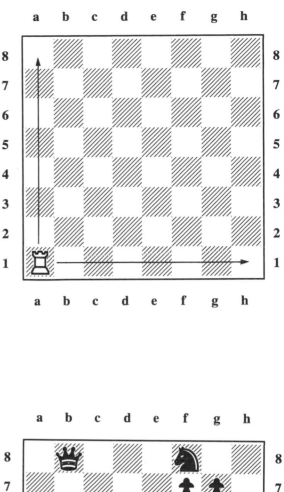

The first plays are:

1 Rc2 × c5

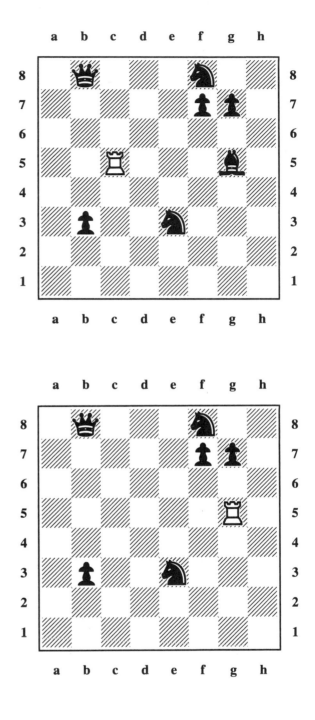

2 Rc5 × g5

Can you work the rest out? Try now, without looking at the answer below.

———————————————

Solution: **Rg5 × g7 × f7 × f8 × b8 × b3 × e3**

NOW ANOTHER ONE

This time there are 10 enemy pieces. Try to work it out before you begin. Remember, you must take one enemy piece with each move until there are none left.

———————

Solution: Rc2 × c5 × g5 × g7 × f7 × f8 × b8 × b3 × e3 × h3 × h1

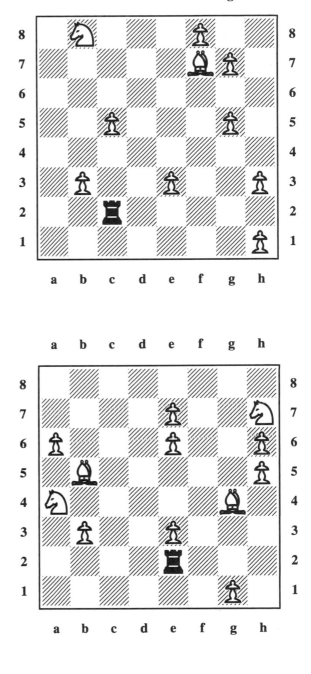

AND YET ANOTHER

And now you have to take 12 enemy pieces. Are you up to it? Try to think 12 moves ahead first. It's not so difficult. Remember, you must take an enemy piece first.

———————

Solution: Re2 × e3 × b3 × b5 × h5 × h6 × h7 × e7 × e6 × a6 × a4 × g4 × g1

♞ THE ♞
KNIGHT

A horse! a horse! my kingdom for a horse!
Shakespeare—*Richard III*

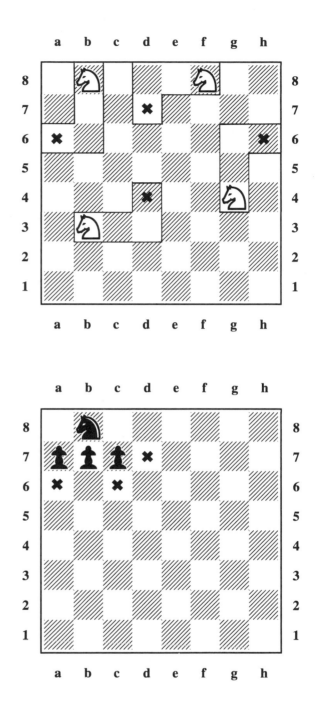

The German word *Springer* is probably the world's best name for the knight. *Springer* means jumper, and the knight is the only piece that can jump over other pieces.

The knight moves in an L-shape but he takes only on the square where he finishes his jump.

Here, the knight can jump over the pawns and take any piece on **a6**, **c6** or **d7**.

Note: The symbol for knight is N because K is used for king.

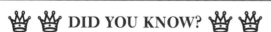

The knights here can go to the squares marked. With each jump, a knight moves from a white to a black square, or from black to white. Always it is like this: first two squares forward or backwards or sideways, and then right or left one more square. With your finger, trace the L-shaped paths the knights take to the marked squares.

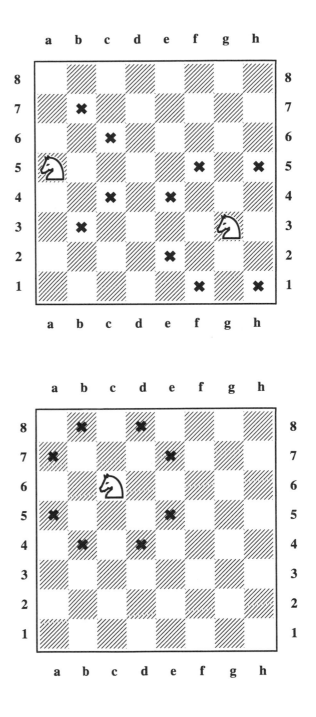

The Starship Knight

James McMahan, the young captain of the W.S.S. *Armstrong*, was in trouble. His ship had been attacked in a remote part of the galaxy. Now here he was with his crew of sixteen, prisoners on Procyon V.

His blurred senses took in the situation. He was in a large room. His crew, suspended in clear tubes lining one wall, were also just regaining consciousness. Several Cyonites, humanoid creatures with mottled grey skin, stood nearby. One turned and spoke to him with the aid of a standard translator pack. The Cyonite was offering one chance. A challenge. If McMahan won, they would go free, if not . . .

The room's lighting dimmed and a gigantic glowing chessboard appeared on one wall. Only the sixteen white pieces showed. McMahan understood. He looked at his trapped crew. Each piece lost meant . . . The tense face of Gaia, his first officer, was turned towards the board. He could see that she, too, understood that their lives were at stake.

In place of the black pieces, the Cyonite was to have only one piece. This mystery piece would remain invisible, but it would move in a definite pattern. The Cyonite led him to a gleaming control panel. McMahan swallowed hard. He did not want to lose a single crew member. Cautiously he pressed a button which moved a pawn forward on the giant board. Lights flashed as his opponent answered immediately.

The white position took shape. Beads of sweat glimmered on McMahan's forehead.

The human brain contains more cells than there are are stars in the universe, and it seemed as if he was using them all. Would they be enough? He glanced at his first officer. Gaia was pounding against the tube, but there was no sound.

Suddenly a yellow light bathed the board and a white pawn disappeared. McMahan spun around to see his ship's engineer dissolve into nothingness.

Gaia began pounding frantically against the tube wall. James McMahan trembled. He gripped the control panel hard and brought his concentration back to the board. He had to think. Something was nagging at the back of his mind. He felt the answer to the mystery piece that was touring the board was very near. He glanced again at his first officer, still pounding silently. K–N–

He knew! Quickly he took in the board. A piece was threatened. He moved it. Then, when the flashing lights signalled that the mystery piece had made its move, James McMahan was ready. He slanted his bishop across the board and pounced. The room lights came up. The giant chessboard was no more. McMahan blinked. He had won! "Take them to their ship," the Cyonite ordered. James McMahan breathed a sigh of relief, then grinned as chief engineer Rodham rematerialized and all the tubes opened wide to release the happy crew.

As Procyon V faded away on the viewscreen to become just one star among many, James McMahan held a book that had been brought from the ship's library. It was old and the pages were yellowed. It was H. J. Murray's *A History of Chess*, written back in the twentieth century. In it Murray describes the Knight's Tour, a problem in which the knight visits every square of the chessboard without covering any square more than once. Impishly James McMahan looked at his first officer. "By the time I realized you were pounding in code, I had just about figured it out myself," he said. "I'm afraid I didn't care to wait that long, Captain," replied Gaia with a half smile. "I might have been next." Then she joined him in laughter, the laughter of life.

Photo by Gary Moyes, London

The Knight's Driving Test

To pass your test, your white knight has to take all the black pawns, which are fixed and do not move. It can be done in eighteen moves, but as long as you do it, the number of moves is not important.

Here is one way of doing it.

1 Ng1 – f3

2 Nf3 – g5

He is making for the outside pawn at **h7**.

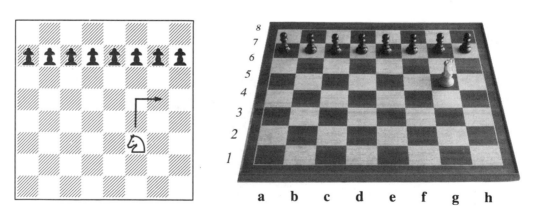

3 Ng5 × h7

4 Nh7 – g5

5 Ng5 × f7

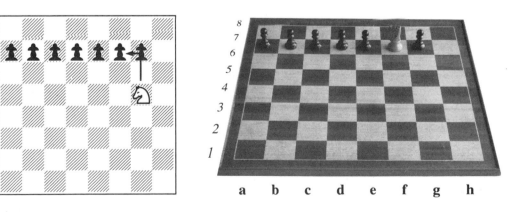

6 Nf7 – e5

7 Ne5 × d7

8 Nd7 – c5

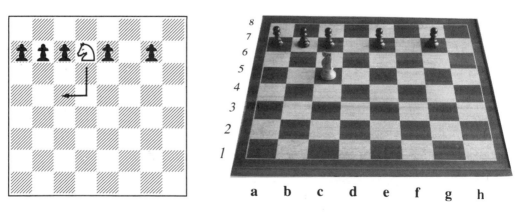

9 Nc5 × b7

Next comes a tricky three-point turn to get the knight to take the outside pawn on **a7**.

10 Nb7 – a5

11 Na5 – c6

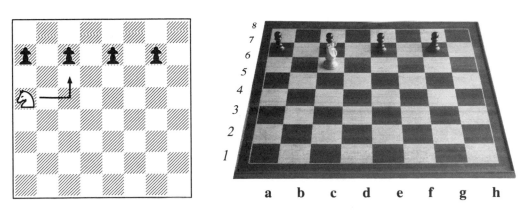

12 Nc6 × a7

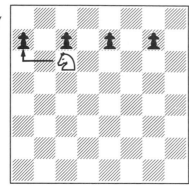

From this point it's easy. The knight comes back to **b5** and then captures the pawn on **c7**.

Then it comes back to **d5** and then captures the pawn on **e7**, and then there is only the last one to do. Can you do it?

This is not the only way to do the driving test in eighteen moves. But it is impossible to do it in fewer moves. Can you do it this way by yourself and then find other ways?

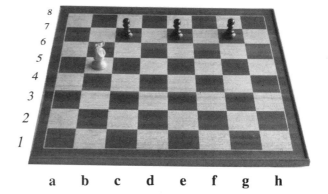

After you pass the Knight's Driving Test, you can have a certificate showing that you did it! Make a copy of the blank certificate form at the back of the book, and have someone fill it out for you.

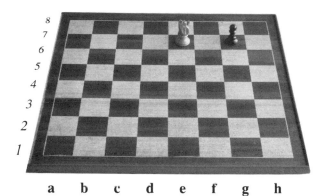

ADVANCED DRIVING TEST

For this advanced driving test you must start by taking the pawn on **a7** first and you have to take all the pawns in nineteen moves. Let's see you work it out yourself.

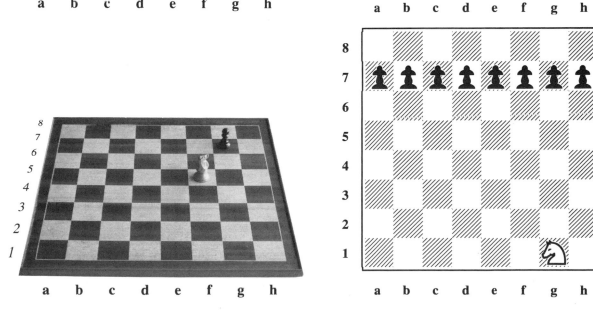

THE KING

Ay, every inch a King,

Shakespeare—*King Lear*

Although the king is the most important piece in a game of chess, its move is very limited. It can go in any direction, forward, backwards, to the sides, or diagonally, but *only one square at a time*.

Can you go from **h1** to **h5** in only four moves? Yes, it's easy. Go straight up the board, **h2**, **h3**, **h4**, **h5**. Nothing could be simpler. But now, try getting the king from **h1** to **h5** in four moves while passing over a square on the "f" file as well. Can you do it?

———

Solution: g2 – f3 – g4 – h5

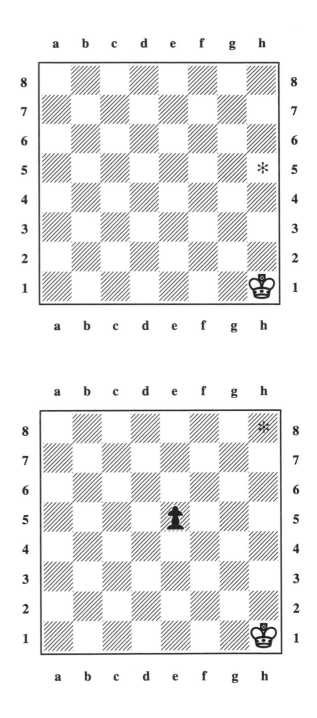

Now of course it's easy to get from **h1** to **h8** in seven moves. You just go **h2**, **h3**, **h4**, **h5**, **h6**, **h7**, **h8**. But can you do it in seven moves and still take the pawn on **e5**?

The Duel of the Kings

The starting position for each king is at the end of the "e" file. The winner of this game is the first king to reach the other side.

Neither king can move to any of the three squares marked NO. They are contested by the opposing king.

Rule: When you play chess, if by some chance or oversight you make a move leaving the king on a square where it is being attacked, you must put the position back to the way it was before the oversight and must play a different, legal move.

♖ ♖ **DID YOU KNOW?** ♖ ♖

The start of the James Bond film *From Russia With Love* was set at a Moscow chess championship. The final position shown on the demonstration boards is one actually played by Spassky against Bronstein in 1959 at Leningrad (now St. Petersburg).

The King and Pawn Game

White starts, as in every game of chess. If you want to win, advance your king quickly and get him to capture the enemy pawns.

The king cannot go onto any of the squares marked NO because he would be moving into check.

PART THREE

CHESS RULES AND THE FULL BOARD

Check

Our word "checkmate" is from the Persian words "shah mat," which mean "the king is dead." "Shah mat" was said in many countries and through many hundreds of years until, in English, it became checkmate. Surround and attack the king—that is the final aim of chess.

Check is simply a position where the king can be captured.

White king in check to black rook.

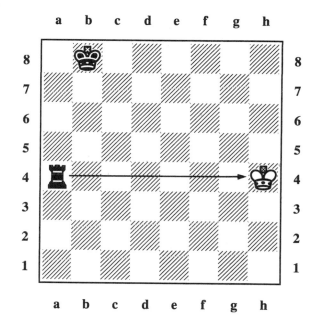

White king in check to black bishop.

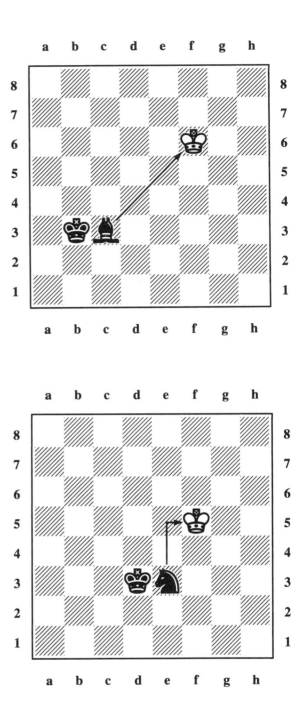

White king in check to black knight.

White king in check to black queen.

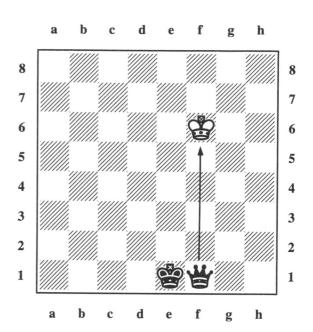

If your king is in check, you must stop this on the next move. There are three ways for you to do this:

- Move the king to a safe square.
- Put one of your pieces in the way of the check. This is called "blocking."
- Capture the attacker.

School chess club students match up on South Lincolnshire playground.

Here are three illustrated examples of check, and how to get out of check:

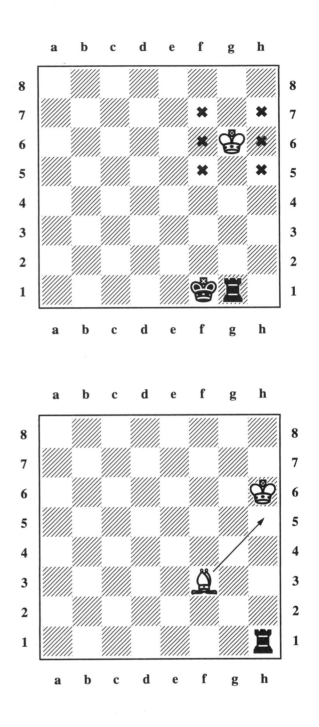

1. Simply move the king out of the way of the rook's line of attack to any one of the squares marked.

2. Block the check by moving the bishop to stand in the line of the rook's line of attack.

3. This time, easily the best way to get out of check is to take the checking piece.

Some of the more than 3,600 players taking part in 1988 chess tournament in Hamburg, Germany.

Staatliche Landesbildstelle, Hamburg. Courtesy of Gert Blankenburg

Checkmate

If the king cannot escape, then of course it is checkmate. The game is over.

The white queen checks the black king. The king's way off of the back rank is blocked by the white king. It is checkmate.

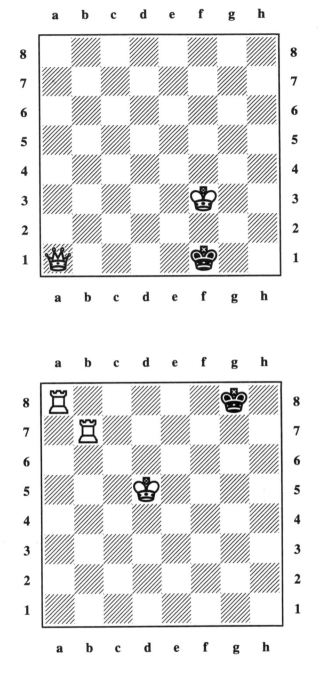

One of the white rooks gives check. This time the king cannot escape onto the next rank, which is guarded by the other white rook. This is checkmate.

CHECKMATE QUIZ

Here are twelve chances to try your hand at checkmating:

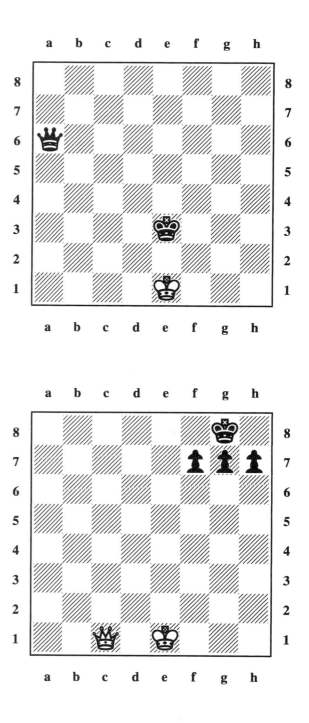

1. Black to move. There are two different ways to checkmate the white king.

2. White to move. A back rank checkmate.

3. White to move. The queen needs the bishop's protection to give checkmate.

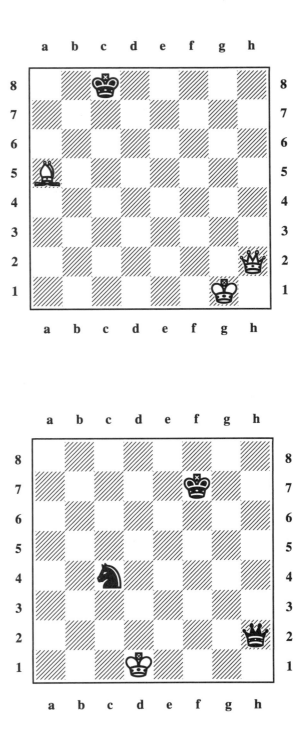

4. Black to move. The queen and knight link up to give checkmate.

5. Black to move. Another queen-and-knight double act to give checkmate.

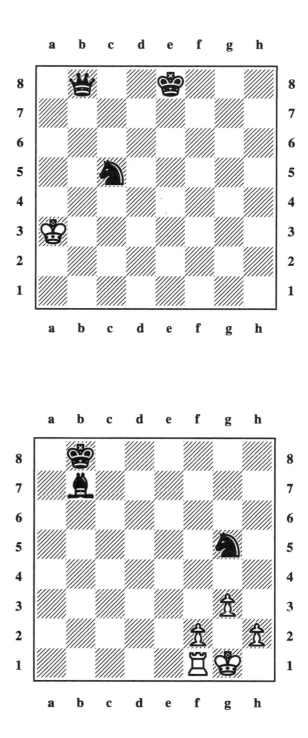

6. Black to move. The bishop covers two of the white king's escape squares. The knight moves in to give checkmate.

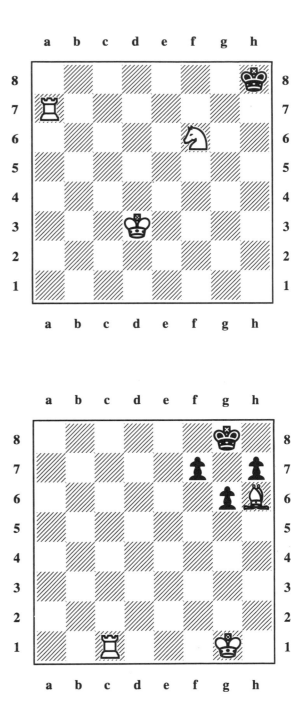

7. White to move. The knight helps the rook to give checkmate.

8. White to move. The bishop hems in the black king. The rook moves in to give checkmate.

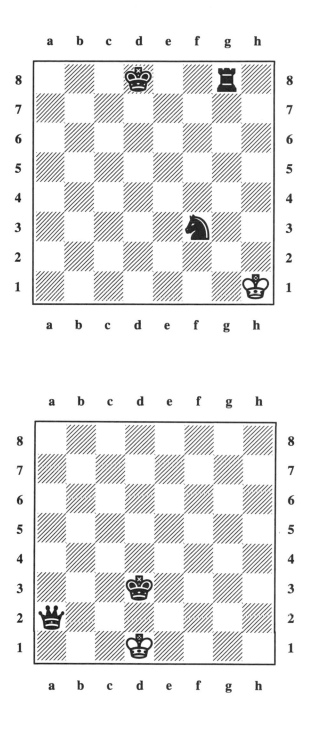

9. Black to move. The knight helps the rook to give checkmate.

10. The queen checkmates with the help of the black king.

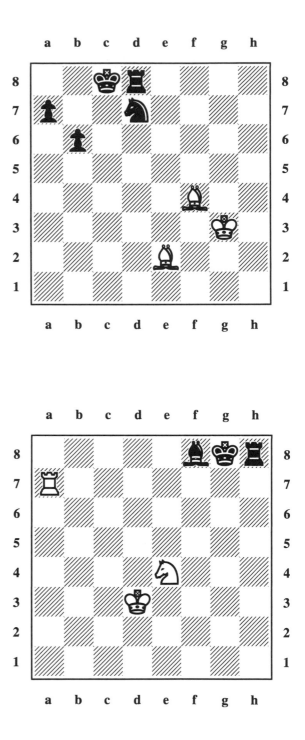

11. One white bishop cuts off the black king. The other moves in to give checkmate.

12. The knight moves in to give checkmate to the black king. The white rook prevents any escape.

The Raging Rooks of Harlem are popular opponents at Central Park Chessathon.

CHECKMATE QUIZ SOLUTIONS

1. **Qe2 mate or Qa1 mate**
2. **Qc8 mate**
3. **Qc7 mate**
4. **Qd2 mate**
5. **Qb3 mate**
6. **Nh3 mate**
7. **Rh7 mate**
8. **Rc8 mate**
9. **Rg1 mate**
10. **Qd2 mate or Qa1 mate or Qb1 mate**
11. **Ba6 mate**
12. **Nf6 mate**

♖ ♖ **DID YOU KNOW?** ♖ ♖

Star Trek's Captain Kirk and his first officer, Mister Spock, played a form of three-dimensional chess on the Starship *Enterprise* in the 1966 episode "Charlie X."

Sarah plays one of her rooks in a full game.

Parade of the Pieces

It was holiday time. The square was crowded except for the large roped-off area in the middle. Banners fluttered in the breeze. The band played stirring marches for the waiting crowds. The mayor sat high above the crowd in a tennis umpire's chair. The town's football coach, surrounded by fans, sat facing him across the space which was marked out as a giant chessboard. Six trumpeters stood poised across the entrance to the square. Behind them, costumed live chess pieces lined up for their entrances.

The Master of Ceremonies gave a signal. The trumpets sounded and the trumpeters stepped aside. The procession started to move. Frantically, a little boy tugged at the mayor's long robe. "The board's the wrong way around," he whispered loudly. The mayor looked at the nearest right-hand corner square. He went pale. It was black. He looked at the his adviser. "Does it matter?" he asked. "It's the rule, sir. Players must have white corner squares nearest their right hands." The mayor gestured to the traffic officer, who raised a hand and stopped the procession. The mayor climbed down from his seat. "Shift the chairs to those sides, please."

Once again the trumpets sounded. The procession moved forward. First, riding on motorcycles, came four rooks, two with white castle-like battlements around them, two with black. The rooks were directed to the corner squares.

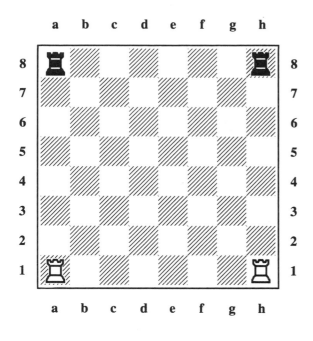

Then four knights on horseback were guided by their squires to the squares next to the rooks.

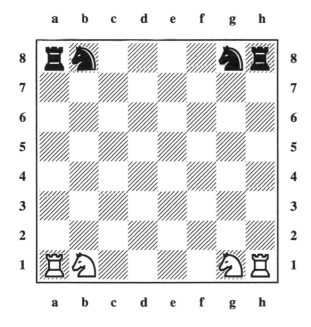

The four bishops walked solemnly in single file to the middle of the board before dispersing to the squares next to the knights.

Another fanfare of trumpets. This time the black queen arrived in a gleaming black, small but powerful sports car. The traffic officer looked uncertain which square to direct her to. The little boy spoke up confidently, "The queen always starts on a square of her own color. Black queen—black square." The queen was motioned on.

Trumpets sounded again. This time it was easy to guide the white queen, in her own shiny white car, to her white square.

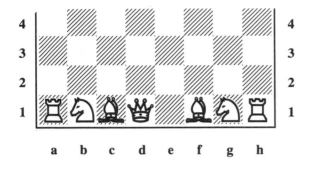

Again the fanfare. The black king, robed and attended by his pages, strode to the remaining back-row square. His forces bowed low in honor.

Now the white king made his entrance and acknowledged the salutes.

With the courts of both sides in position, the two kings ordered their pawns, eight white and eight black, to march in and take their places in the rows before them.

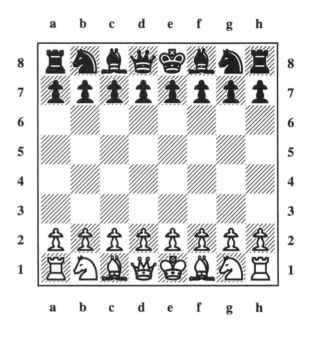

The game was ready to begin. The ambulance attendants moved to the wings, ready to remove the casualties. The band played the national anthem. The public address system crackled into life. The crowd grew quiet.

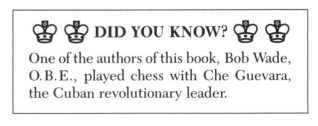

♚ ♚ DID YOU KNOW? ♚ ♚

One of the authors of this book, Bob Wade, O.B.E., played chess with Che Guevara, the Cuban revolutionary leader.

The mayor, of course, had to make the first move. White always starts first. "My 'e' pawn two squares forward, please," he called out, and the game had begun.

The game went on all afternoon with jeers and cheers following the moves. Finally, as the sun dipped low, the board was cleared of all but the two kings. It was an honorable draw.

Young chess player at Chessathon.

U.S. Chess Federation, New Windsor, NY

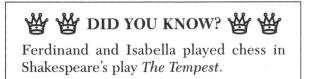

DID YOU KNOW?
Ferdinand and Isabella played chess in Shakespeare's play *The Tempest.*

Two Last Rules

CASTLING

Now that you know the moves of the king and rook, it is time for you to learn a very special move, in which two pieces move at the same time. In the Middle Ages, the players decided the king was safer in the corner of the board, and they had a move called the "King's Leap" which took the king to safety.

Later, in the fourteenth and fifteenth centuries, "castling" was introduced. This, and the new moves of the queen and bishop, added new dimensions to the game. What is castling?

When you castle you do two things. First, you play your king two squares along the back rank towards a rook. Then, with the rook, you jump over the king onto the next square. *This all counts as one move.*

You can castle towards either rook. Castling towards the rook on the right is called castling kingside (the side of the board the king stands on), or a short castle. In algebraic notation it looks like this: **0-0**. Castling towards the left is called castling queenside, or a long castle. In notation, it is written as **0-0-0**.

Before castling kingside.

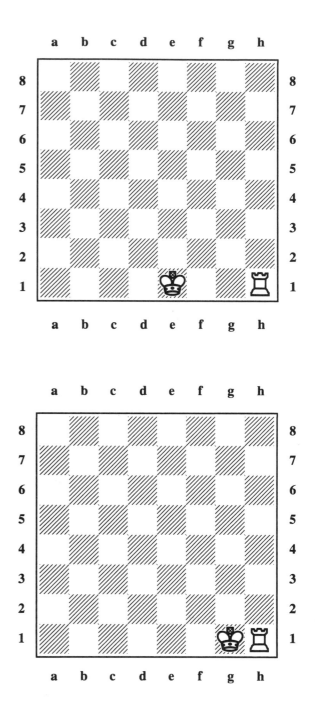

The king moves two squares towards the rook.

The rook moves over the top of the king to the square on the other side. This is castling.

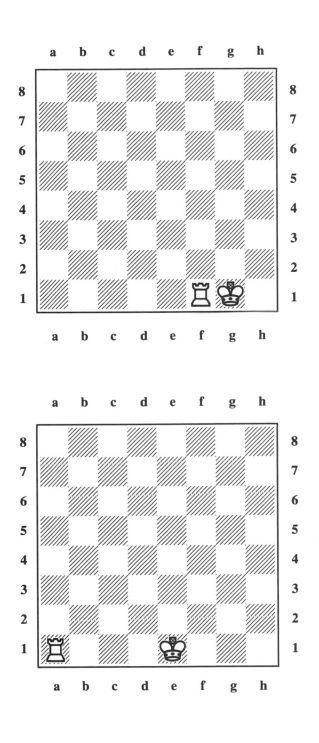

Before castling queenside.

The king moves two squares towards the rook, which moves to the other side of the king.

Black castles kingside.

Black castles queenside.

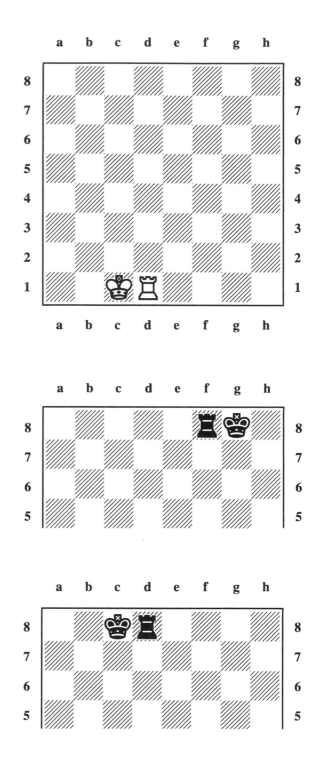

You **cannot** castle:

1. If the king or the rook has moved.
2. If there is a piece between the king and the rook.
3. If the king is in check.
4. If the king finishes the move in check.
5. If the king passes over a square that is attacked by an enemy piece. This is a difficult one, so here are four examples.

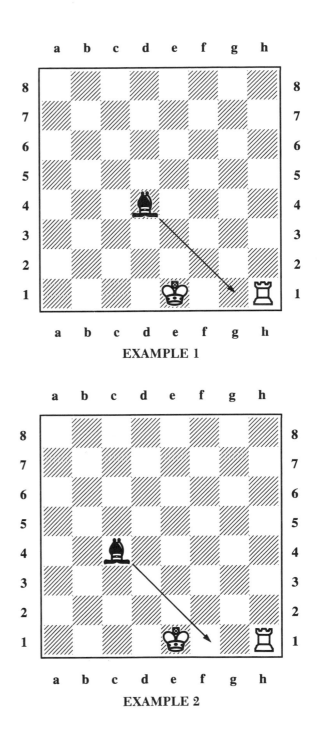

EXAMPLE 1

EXAMPLE 2

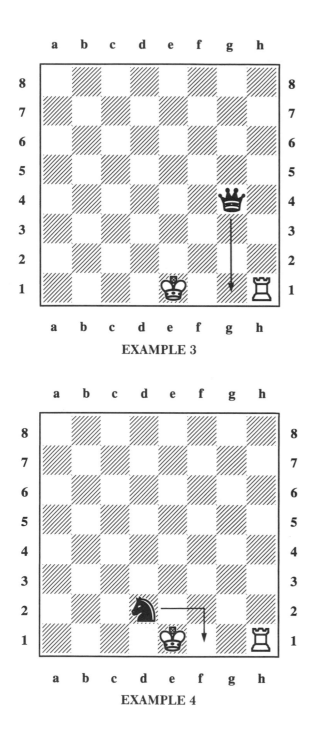

EXAMPLE 3

EXAMPLE 4

♞ ♞ DID YOU KNOW? ♞ ♞

Chess players helped sink a ship.

It was during World War II. The German battleship *Bismarck* was somewhere in the mid-Atlantic, a "needle in a haystack."

British Prime Minister Churchill ordered the radio dispatches from Berlin monitored. When a coded signal to the ship came through, he called on four of his expert code breakers. Two of them were Britain's top chess players Hugh Alexander and P.S. Milner-Barry. With the help of another top player, Harry Golombek, the code was broken, the ship was located, and the Royal Navy sank the *Bismarck*.

EN PASSANT

There is one more, final rule for you to understand—a special pawn move called *en passant*, French for "in passing." It was made to stop the game from becoming blocked by pawn barriers.

Here is the rule. If you move your pawn two squares on the opening move, I am allowed to push it back one square and take it with one of my own pawns if I am able. But I *must* do it on the *immediately following* move.

If black advances the "b" pawn *one* square, the white pawn can take it.

The "b" pawn advances *two* squares, from **b7** to **b5**. My "c" pawn can still take it. But it must be done *this* move.

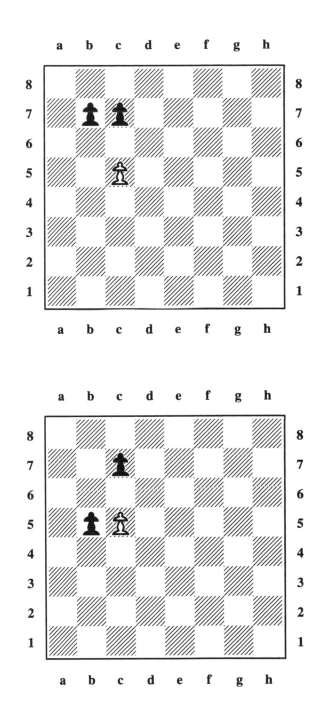

```
👑 👑 DID YOU KNOW? 👑 👑
```

Chris Bonington, the brilliant mountaineer, played chess in the Himalayas at an altitude of 20,000 feet. Another lover of chess under cold conditions was Robert Falcon Scott, explorer of the Antarctic.

First, I push black's pawn back one square to **b6**.

Then, as part of the same move, I take it.

Repeat: My opponent's pawn moves two squares. The very next move, I push it back one square so that my pawn can, and does, take it.

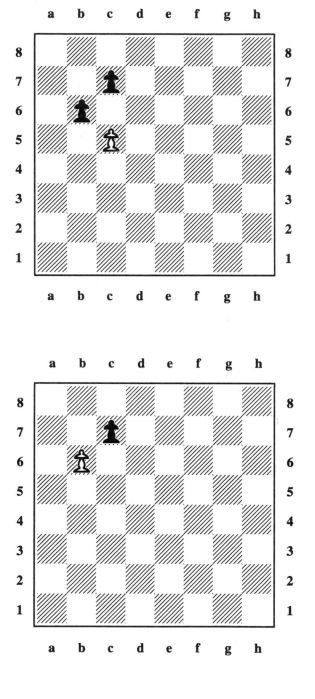

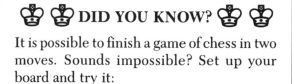 DID YOU KNOW?

It is possible to finish a game of chess in two moves. Sounds impossible? Set up your board and try it:

1	f2 – f3	e7 – e5
2	g2 – g4	Qd8 – h4

Drawn Games

If you can't win, play for a draw. The scoring system in chess is one point for a win, half a point for a draw, and nothing for a loss. But to finish up in a draw after a long hard struggle is often more satisfying than to win an easy game.

Here are some endings where checkmate cannot be given. These endings are drawn.

King versus king.
This is a draw.

King and knight against king.
This also is drawn because the king and knight cannot on their own give checkmate.

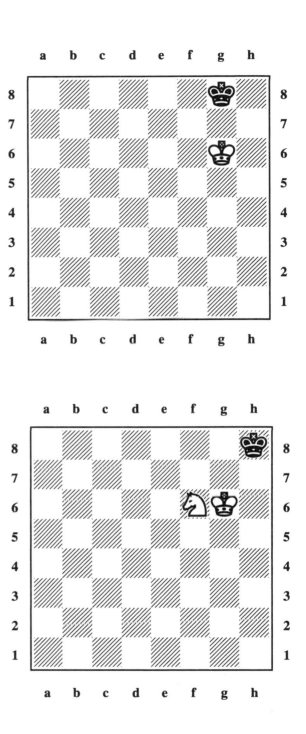

King and bishop against king cannot give checkmate.

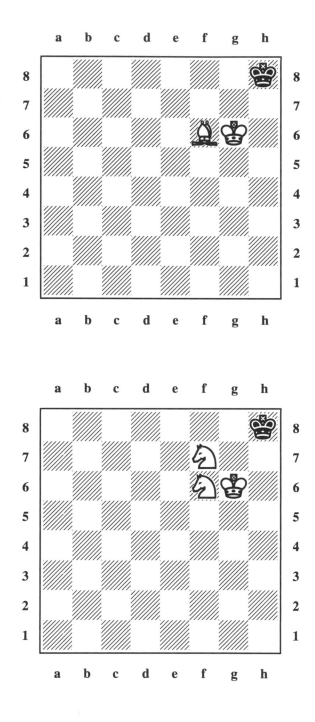

As this shows, the two white knights can give checkmate if the black king allows it. But, as long as the black king keeps out of the corner, it is not possible for the two knights to give checkmate. The king and two knights can only draw.

How else are draws agreed upon by the two players?

- By stalemate.
- By the fifty-move rule.
- By repeating the position three times.
- By perpetual check.

STALEMATE

When you have an overwhelming force and you allow a stalemate to happen, you feel very foolish!

In the examples here, the king is not in check, but every square to which he can move will be check. This is stalemate.

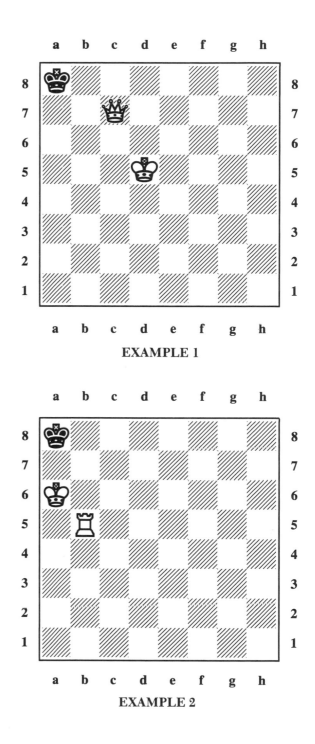

EXAMPLE 1

EXAMPLE 2

♟ ♟ **DID YOU KNOW?** ♟ ♟

Chess was involved with the discovery of America. In 1492, when Columbus sought ships from King Ferdinand for his journey to the New World, it is said that he was granted them because the King was in a good mood from winning at chess.

FIFTY-MOVE RULE

Either player can claim a draw if there have been fifty moves without any pawn moves or any captures. If there are pawn moves or captures then you must start counting again. This rule usually comes into force when you have to checkmate the enemy king with a king and a queen, or a king and a rook or some such combination. You have to deliver the checkmate in fifty moves or else it is a draw.

REPEATED POSITION

Even the world's great players have made mistakes over this rule, when to claim a draw, so let's get it clear right now.

If the identical position on the board, that is the same pieces on the same squares with the same player to move, *happens or is about to happen three times*, then the one whose turn it is to move may claim a draw.

PERPETUAL CHECK

White is losing but the white queen can give check forever (this is the meaning of *perpetual* check) on **e8** and **h5**. This is a draw.

David Gertler takes on a young participant at New York Chessathon.

PART FOUR

GREAT GAMES AND PLAYERS

When the Rules Changed

This is something to beware of when you start playing chess. If you are not careful, your enemy's queen and bishop can finish off the game in four moves. If someone from the Court of Haroun al-Rashid, one of the famous Caliphs of Baghdad, travelled through time to see the modern game, this is one of the things that would most shock him. For his queen—only to him it was a minister, not a queen—moved only one square at a time diagonally. His bishop moved two squares diagonally. But where play in his time took ages for opponents to come to grips at chess (pawns did not even have the privilege of moving two squares on the first move), now, in four flashing moves, it is possible to checkmate! How did this happen?

Somewhere between the twelfth and fourteenth centuries, during the time of the Crusading Knights, a rule change occurred. It enabled the queen to move anywhere (no wonder the new queen was called "mad"), and the bishop to move as many squares as he liked along the diagonals of the board.

Here's a story of what might have happened when Richard the Lionheart and Saladin, leader of the Saracens, sat down at the chessboard to play under the new rules.

1   e2 – e4

1 . . . . . e7 – e5

2 Qd1 – h5

A beginner's move now: but a very strong move by Richard under the new rule change. This early queen sortie is not recommended, even though it may lead to wins against other beginners.

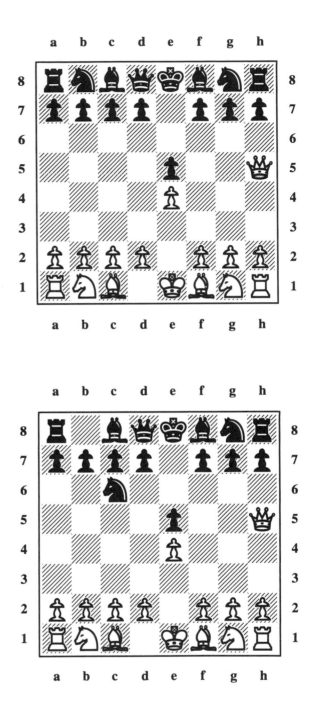

2 ..... Nb8 – c6

Saladin's knight move hasn't changed over the years.

3 Bf1 – c4

Instead of only two squares diagonally, the bishop can now move diagonally as many squares as it likes under the new rule change. Now Richard's queen and bishop attack the weak spot, **f7**.

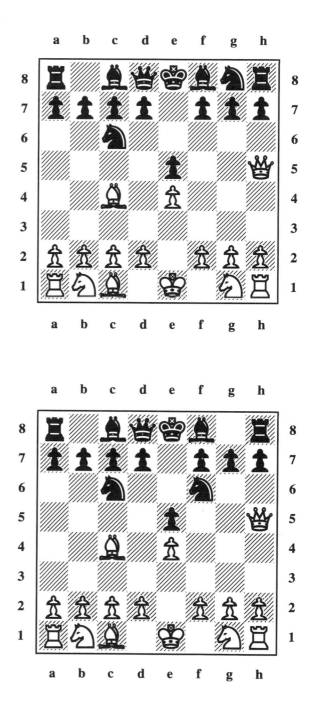

3 . . . . . Ng8 – f6

Unused to this play, Saladin fails to spot this danger.

4 Qh5 × f7 checkmate.

Checkmate. The game is over already. Having once seen checkmate delivered in four flashing moves, let's see how Saladin's advisers stopped it.

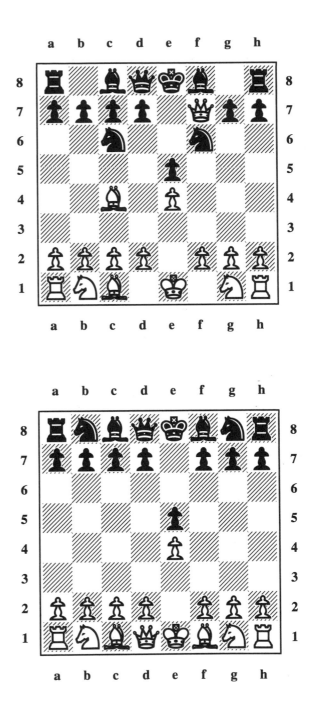

SALADIN'S DEFENSE

All night long, Saladin's advisers worked on the defense to this new manner of play. It had ruined chess as they knew it. Now it was urgent that they work out a defense that would give them back their self-respect. There was much to-ing and fro-ing and coming and going, but soon Saladin was shown the results of their labors.

Saladin and his advisers surround the board.

1 e2 – e4

1 . . . . . e7 – e5

The game starts as before.

2 Qd1 – h5

2 ..... Nb8 – c6

His advisers tell Saladin that there is no
point at all in giving away the king's pawn at
e5. Besides, this knight is now out and would
be very useful soon.

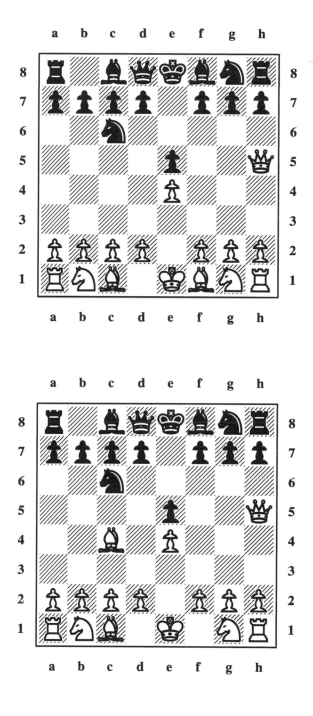

3 Bf1 – c4

Out comes the bishop. Saladin's face
pales. Is he to be checkmated by this ac-
cursed queen again?

3 ..... g7 – g6

The Grand Vizier leans forward and moves a pawn. Saladin can now see that the queen's path is blocked.

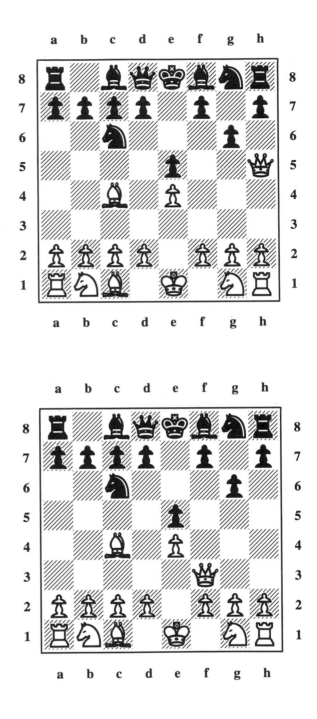

4 Qh5 – f3

Retreat is the order of the day. Saladin smiles. But checkmate by **Q × f7** is still threatened. Saladin is worried again when he sees this.

4 ..... Ng8 – f6

The knight blocks the checkmate.

5 g2 – g4

His advisers tell Saladin that the Crusader will surely advance this pawn to attack the knight and so clear the way for the white queen to checkmate. "Do not worry," they assure him, "we have the answer."

5 ..... Nc6 – d4

This knight counterattacks by striking at the white queen. The queen has to move.

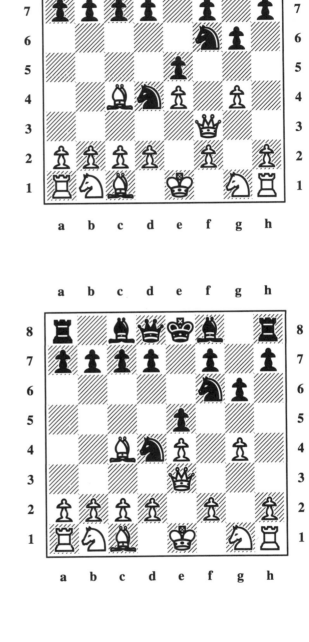

6 Qf3 – e3

Saladin now sees what his advisers have ready.

6 . . . . . Nd4 × c2 check.

A royal family fork attacking king, queen, and rook. Saladin's face is wreathed in smiles. He is ready for Richard's return visit. Tonight he will have his revenge.

Jason Rosehaws of 1991 U.S. amateur team studies his position.

Paul Morphy

The elements so mix'd in him
that Nature might stand up
And say to all the world,
"This was a man!"

Shakespeare—*Julius Caesar*

Paul Morphy was a young man of genius who played striking chess with a very attacking style. He returned from Europe at the age of twenty-one as virtual world champion, becoming the first All-American hero. He is the most famous player in chess history.

Morphy was born in 1837 into one of the most well-known families in the southern states of America. He learned to play at the age of ten by watching his father and uncle at the board.

At the age of nineteen he attended and easily won the first American championship. It was clear he was somebody special and it was arranged that he should travel to England to play Howard Staunton, who was then the acknowledged king of chess.

Staunton, a famous columnist and Shakespeare commentator, would not play Morphy. It is certain that he realized he would lose if he did.

Frustrated by Staunton's refusal to play a match (they did play friendly games at Staunton's country house outside London), Morphy left for Paris to play Daniel Harrwitz and Adolf Anderssen, the best players in Europe. Morphy beat them both easily.

He returned to America as the best player in the world and received a hero's welcome. He was the first American to take Europe on and conquer. The steamships tooted their

Paul Morphy's monogram adorns the goblets of this silver pitcher set in the U.S. Chess Federation Hall of Fame.

horns as his ship returned up the Hudson River and the papers were full of him for months.

It is one of his games that he played in Paris that we give you now. It was played in 1858 at the Paris Opera House. His two opponents insisted that he sit with his back to the opera, one that he very much wanted to see, so that he could "really concentrate!" This exquisite game was the result.

♖ ♖ DID YOU KNOW? ♖ ♖

They love chess in Iceland. The British player Nigel Short is one of the most popular personalities there. In a poll he came in second, above Madonna.

Chess great Paul Morphy.

PHILIDOR'S DEFENSE

The chief idea in chess is to get the pieces out quickly and into active play. You cannot attack, let alone try to checkmate, with one or two pieces. You must develop all of them as each piece has a job to do. A good way to begin is to release two pieces at one go. This can be done by advancing one of the middle pawns. Morphy, in this game, shows us all how to get the pieces out and off the back rank. Set up a board for a full game, and recreate with us this historic game.

♗ ♗ **DID YOU KNOW?** ♗ ♗

The 1993 movie *Searching for Bobby Fischer* is about a young prodigy making his way up in the chess world through the system of competitions.

PARIS OPERA HOUSE, 1858

WHITE	**BLACK**
Paul Morphy	The Duke of Brunswick and the Count of Isouard

1 e2 – e4

1 . . . . . e7 – e5

The two aristocrats know at least this: that they must fight for the center of the board. They know that pieces placed in the center have the greatest freedom of action. As you will see, Morphy's grasp of this idea is unmatched.

2 Ng1 – f3

It is difficult to improve on this move. As the knight comes out it attacks the black pawn in the center. Morphy gains time because black is not free to do as he pleases. The two aristocrats must save the pawn. Morphy loves to bring out his pieces with a threat and so gain time. It is a feature of his play in this game.

2 . . . . . d7 – d6

The move to **d6**, with a pawn on **e5**, is Philidor's Defense. It does, however, limit the power of their bishop on **f8**, their king bishop or the bishop on the king side. In this game, this bishop never comes to life.

3 d2 – d4

Morphy knows that in the opening you should advance one or two center pawns only. This move challenges in the center and lets out his queen bishop, the bishop on **c1**.

3 . . . . . Bc8 – g4

This move pins Morphy's knight because, if he should move it, the bishop will take Morphy's queen.

4 d4 × e5

This is a slight threat. If the aristocrats take back with the pawn, Morphy will exchange queens and with his knight win black's center pawn.

4 . . . . . Bg4 × f3

Never exchange a developed piece for an undeveloped one. This is just what the Duke and the Count do here. Their bishop leaves the field of play. Morphy's queen now comes correctly into the action. He has gained time: his opponents have lost it. Notice Morphy's knight occupied the square **f3** first. Only when his knight was taken did his queen come into play.

5 Qd1 × f3

If you look at your board you will see that the Duke and the Count have no pieces in play, only pawns.

5 . . . . . d6 × e5

Now they can recapture the pawn on their center square.

6 Bf1 – c4

Morphy now has two pieces out to their none and even threatens checkmate. The queen on **f3** can take the pawn on **f7**, protected by the bishop on **c4**, and give checkmate. It is what is called "Scholar's Mate."

This is what Scholar's Mate looks like.

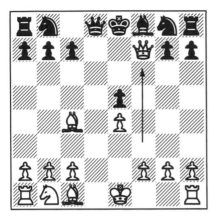

6 ..... Ng8 – f6

The Duke and the Count know they must block this and at last, on their sixth move, a knight comes out.

7   Qf3 – b3

Never move a piece twice in the opening is the rule, but Morphy's queen seeks the most telling square. Here, Morphy supports his bishop in an attack on the black king. The bishop now, with the queen's support,

threatens to take the black pawn on **f7** and give check. The Duke and the Count must stop this. Morphy's queen also threatens the black pawn on **b7**. By making these threats Morphy's pieces are gaining time. The Duke and the Count are restricted in their choice of reply. They must deal with the threats. From now on we provide a diagram for every move, to make Morphy's use of all his pieces even clearer.

7 ..... Qd8 – e7

The aristocrats bring out their queen to stop the attack on their king. But the move is awkward and it stops the bishop from getting into the fray.

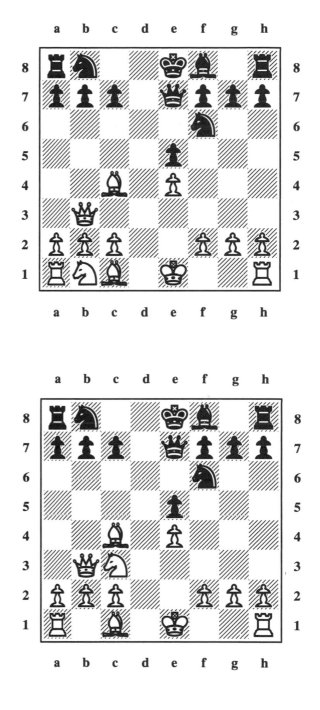

8 Nb1 – c3

Morphy continues to bring his pieces out quickly. His queen could have taken the pawn on **b7**, but Morphy is more concerned with avoiding the trade of queens by ..... **Qe7 – b4** check.

8 ..... c7 – c6

This move protects the pawn on **b7**. The queen now guards it, but the move played does not bring out any pieces. A pawn move is a pawn move. It is not a piece move.

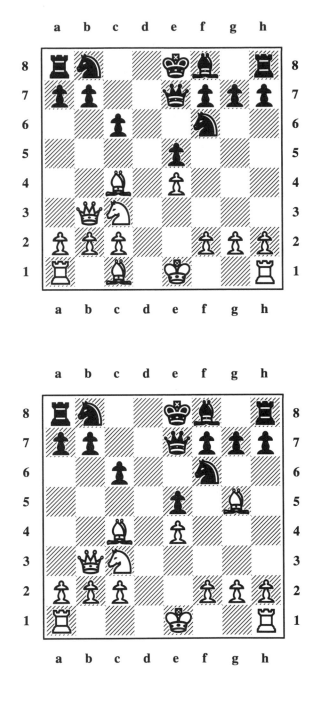

9 Bf1 – g5

Still the pieces race out. This bishop pins the knight on **f6**. If it should move, the bishop will take the queen.

9 ..... b7 – b5

The Duke and the Count hope to drive away Morphy's pieces. They are, however, dangerously short of pieces guarding the king and it is to this that Morphy turns his attention.

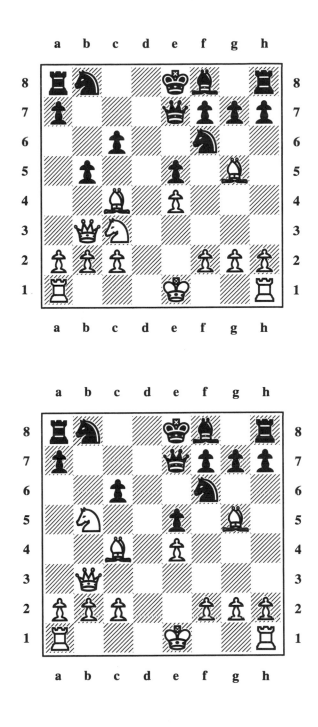

10 Nc3 × b5

Morphy sees the black king still in the center. He knows his pieces are all ready. He judges it correct to sacrifice his knight for an attack on the black king . . . and he's dying to see the opera.

10 ..... c6 × b5

They have to retake. But from now on the attack rolls in. Morphy, it is true, is now a piece down, but he has more pieces in play. It's not who has the most soldiers but who has the most soldiers where the fighting is who will eventually carry the day.

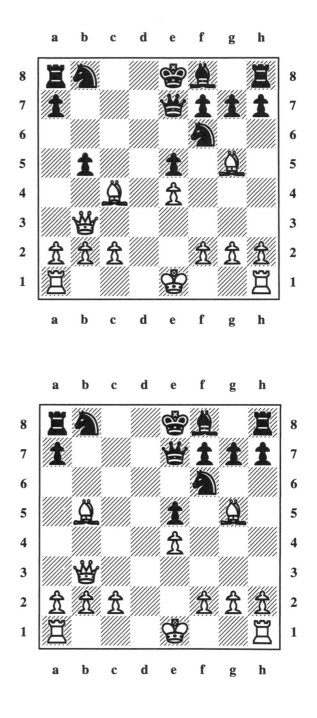

11   Bc4 × b5 check

Now Morphy is ready to pour a Niagara of pieces against the black king, until the tide becomes irresistible.

11 ..... Nb8 – d7

This blocks the check and gets out a piece. Unfortunately, this knight is pinned against the king and cannot move.

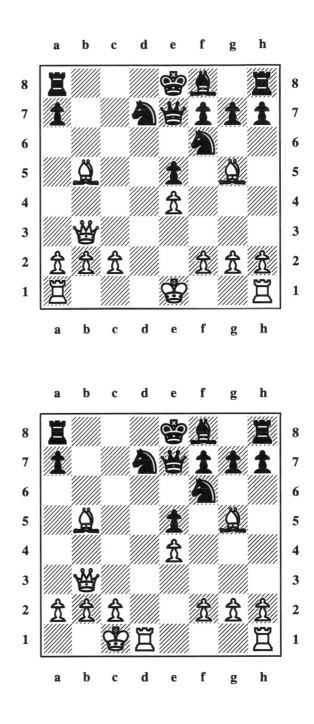

12   0-0-0

Morphy castles long (to queenside) and brings into play a rook against the pinned knight, which is now in trouble with both a rook and a bishop attacking it. The knight is pinned against the king by the bishop and cannot move.

12 ..... Ra8 – d8

This move protects the pinned knight.

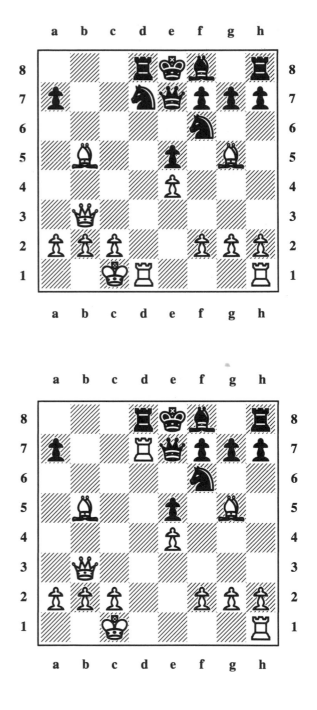

13 Rd1 × d7

Morphy's move will force his opponents to capture with the rook. Their knight is pinned, and now their rook will be pinned onto the king.

13 ..... Rd8 × d7

Notice now that the rook at **d7** cannot move. It would leave their king in check from the bishop. This is called a "pin." Can you see what piece Morphy will bring to attack it?

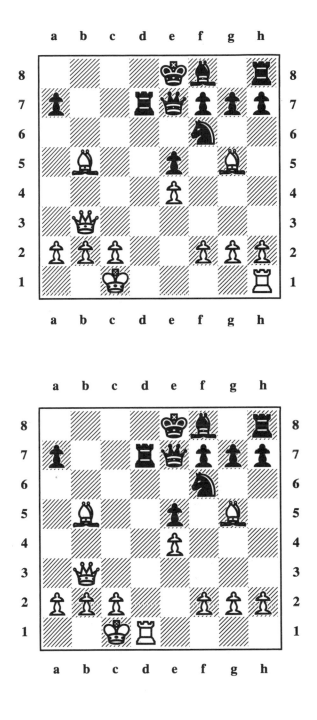

14 Rh1 – d1

Yes, we are sure you got it. Morphy's last piece comes off the bench and straight into an attacking position. The rook on **d7** cannot take Morphy's rook because it is pinned.

14 ..... Qe7 – e6

The queen moves to unpin their knight.
Now the knight protects their rook.

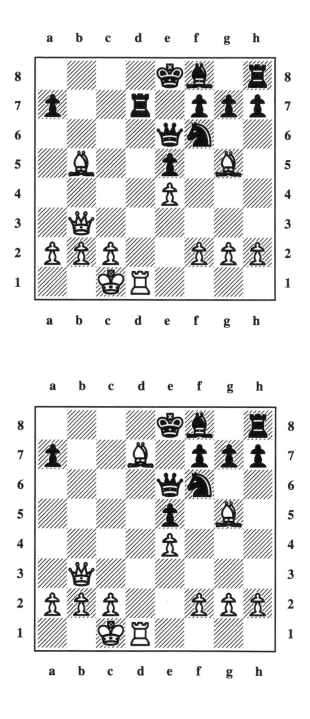

15 Bb5 × d7 check

This clears the way for Morphy's queen to
get to the back rank.

15 ..... Nf6 × d7

The knight can now move and take this checking bishop.

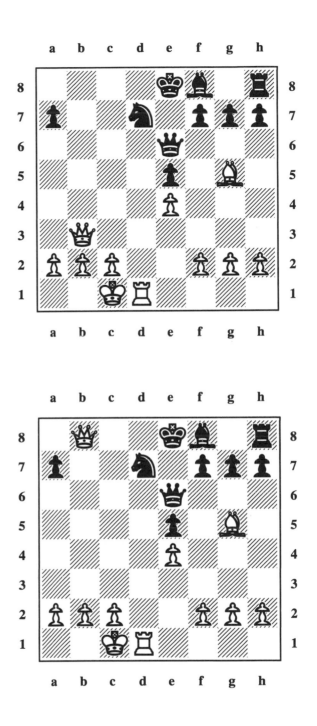

16 Qb3 – b8 check

A brilliant move! But he just wants the knight out of the way so that his rook can deliver checkmate.

16 ..... **Nd7 × b8**

This was forced.

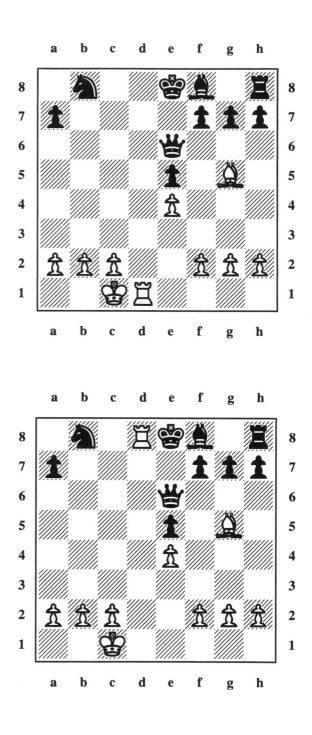

17 **Rd1 – d8** checkmate

What is there to add? Note how all Morphy's pieces took part. Play a game of your own and see if you can get all your pieces into play.

Bobby Fischer

Now is the winter of our discontent
Made glorious summer by this sun of
(New) York.

Shakespeare—*Richard III*

Robert James Fischer, known to everybody as Bobby, learned his chess in the 1950's in New York City. He was about twelve when he, in his own words, "just got good." At the age of thirteen he played a game against Donald Byrne which has since been described as the "Game of the Century." A brilliant move in this game forced Byrne to take Bobby's queen. It also forced Byrne into defeat. It was clear to all who watched him play at the Manhattan Chess Club that Bobby had a marvelous talent. At fourteen he became United States champion, and at fifteen an international grandmaster, at that time the youngest ever in the history of the game.

From the beginning, Bobby did not want to do anything but play chess. At fifteen, just before he qualified as a grandmaster at an international tournament in Yugoslavia, he was taken to see a businessman who offered to pay his expenses and airfare. There was one condition: Bobby had to say that his success was due to the man's help. This Bobby refused to do. Frank Brady, who had gone into the interview with Bobby, said later that he had never been more proud of him.

A month before his nineteenth birthday, Bobby won the World Championship Qualifier Tournament at Stockholm by a clear two

Thirteen-year-old Bobby Fischer plays noted chess instructor John Collins.

and a half points. If he now won at Curaçao he would play for the World Championship. Unfortunately, under the tournament system, which he felt was loaded against him, he did not play well. Bobby's irritation with the World Chess Federation's system got the better of him and the years that followed saw him sidelined.

In 1970, when Bobby was twenty-seven years old, a special match was arranged between the then Soviet Union and the Rest of the World. Bent Larsen of Denmark had been playing very well and had done the grand slam by winning five international tournaments in a row, something which had not been done since Rubinstein's wonderful year in 1911. Larsen was offered the first board in the Rest of the World team. Nobody expected Bobby to play second fiddle to Larsen but he did. He arrived just before the start of the match, glanced briefly at Spassky and Larsen on the first board, sat down, and won his first two games against ex-world champion Petrosian, the man with the best defense in the world. Bobby was back!

It seemed that he was too late to play in the World Championship Qualifying Tournament at Palma de Majorca. However, the American Pal Benko very kindly dropped out and Bobby took his place and romped away with the tournament's first place.

Now a system of knockout matches led the way through to a match with World Champion Boris Spassky. Fischer now astonished the world with resounding 6–0, 6–0 wins against Mark Taimanov and Larsen. The win against Larsen in Denver was truly marvelous, for this was the same Larsen who had played top board for the Rest of the World against the Soviet Union. Counting the wins in the tournament in Palma de Majorca, Bobby had clocked up a winning streak of nineteen consecutive victories against grandmasters!

Bobby now faced Tigran Petrosian in Buenos Aires. Petrosian's style was to force draw after draw until the opponent's patience snapped. He was very good at it. Buenos Aires went wild over Bobby and, to the city's delight, the golden streak continued. Bobby won the first game. Petrosian fought back to win the second game. There followed three draws in a row and Petrosian was now in a match he knew very well. The sixth game was decisive. Bobby won it on the sixty-sixth move. The next game, he won again on the thirty-fourth. Petrosian had cracked. Bobby went on to win the next two games and the match by six and a half points to two and a half. Bobby was now ready for the showdown with the world champion, Boris Spassky. In an interview with BBC Television he called it "this little thing between me and Spassky."

The match, played in Reykjavik, Iceland, captivated the world's press. Shelby Lyman, who covered chess for American Public Service Television, suddenly found himself recognized wherever he went in New York, whether on subway trains or hailing a taxi in the street. The evening Bobby won the match, England's BBC TV made it the number-one item on their world news. Bobby had turned chess into an internationally publicized sport.

On September 2, 1992, at 2:30 P.M. in a superb hotel on a remote island off the coast of Montenegro, Bobby sat down once again to play Boris Spassky. It was as if the years between had never happened.

The world's media were entranced. One of *Time* magazine's leading editors followed the moves avidly and played them on a chessboard in his office causing a lot of amusement among the staff. When Fischer won 10 to 5, the *Times* of London simply said that Fischer was a genius, the Mozart of the sixty-four squares. Bobby is back, everyone said, and it's the start of a new golden age for chess.

THE GAME OF THE CENTURY

It's 1956. Thirteen-year-old Bobby Fischer is playing in the big Lessing Rosenwald tournament in New York against one of America's top chess masters, Donald Byrne. We are at

CHESS REVIEW

the picture chess magazine

MAY 1958

CBS HAD A SECRET

(See Page 132)

50 CENTS

Subscription Rate
ONE YEAR $5.50

Bobby Fischer and Garry Moore, host of television's I've Got a Secret, *on the cover of* Chess Review *magazine in 1958.*

the seventeenth move. Bobby is preparing to sacrifice his queen. The veteran Hans Kmoch, one of New York's most famous chess commentators, calls it, "a move that will be talked about for centuries to come." The queen sacrifice leads to a win in all conceivable variations.

In the thinking that preceded Bobby's move, he had worked out in his head all the possible replies that Byrne could make to the move. He smiled. It did not matter. No matter what Byrne did, in some twenty-odd moves he would be checkmated.

The series of moves that follow is what might have happened if Byrne had *not* taken Bobby's queen on the eighteenth move, but had taken his bishop instead.

1   Bc4 × e6

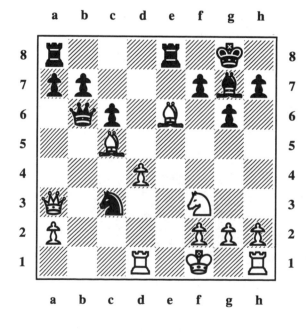

1 . . . . . Qb6 – b5 check

With his black queen still on the board, this would have been Bobby's play.

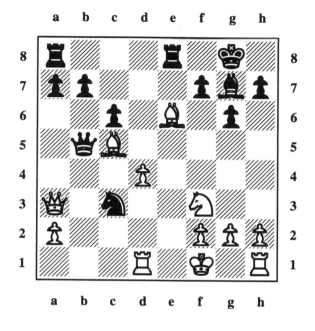

If white plays the king to **e1**, then black would have a simple mate.

2   Kfl – g1

White must make this play.

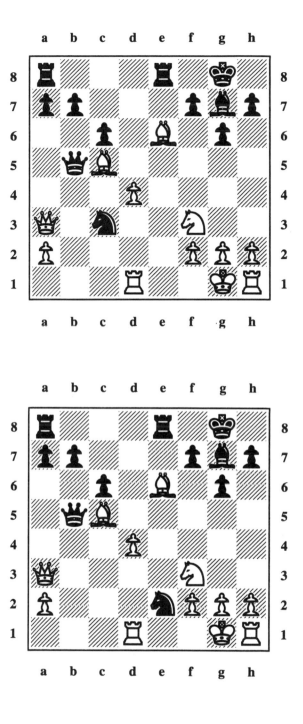

2 . . . . . Nc3 – e2 check

Black would now continue the attack.

3   Kg1 – f1

White must move the threatened king.

Now look carefully. White king and black queen are on the same diagonal. Any knight move would give discovered check. With checkmate in view, Bobby's next play would have been:

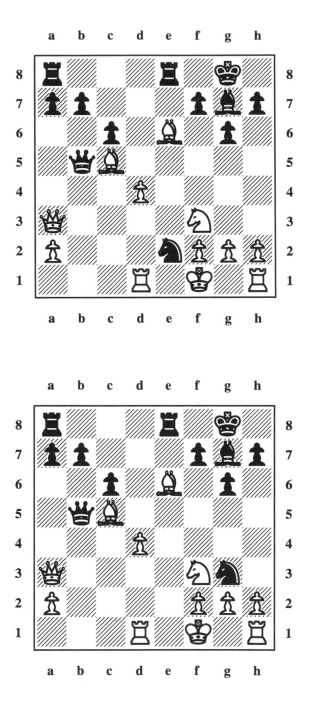

3 ..... **Ne2 – g3** double check

4 Kf1 – g1

White's best move, but it is not good
enough.

4 ..... Qb5 – f1 check

Now Bobby would have played this stun-
ning move. He would lose a queen but get a
checkmate.

5 Rd1 × f1

The king cannot capture. White must use his rook to take the queen.

5 ..... Ng3 – e2 mate!

This is "smothered mate." The white king is smothered by its own pieces.

A Most Extraordinary Finish

The finish in a game of chess can be as exciting as a championship tennis match, a big horse race, or going for the gold in the Olympics.

At Hastings, England, in 1895, Wilhelm Steinitz played a masterpiece against Kurt von Bardeleben. It is one of the most lively, breathtaking games on record. Known as "Steinitz's gem," it deservedly won the brilliancy prize at the tournament and, of course, fully merits its inclusion in so many anthologies of chess games.

Steinitz was the first official world champion. He earned the title when he beat Adolf Anderssen eight games to six in 1866. Paul Morphy had done the same thing, and rather more easily, against a younger Anderssen, but it was agreed in 1866 that the title was now official.

Steinitz remained champion for twenty-eight years, but in 1894 his turn came, as it must to all champions, to lose his title—to the twenty-five-year-old Emanuel Lasker. Chess is now a young person's game, but in all the years from 1866, when Steinitz took the title, to 1921, when Capablanca captured it from Lasker, there were only two world champions. The game was always highly honored. In 1914 Nicholas II, Czar of All the Russias, donated one thousand rubles towards the prize fund of the Saint Petersburg Chess Tournament and declared the top five players "Grandmasters of Chess."

In 1895, although Steinitz was no longer world champion, he produced this lovely game and its startling finish. It assured him permanent inclusion in the Hall of Fame.

	WHITE Steinitz	BLACK Bardeleben
1	e2 – e4	e7 – e5
2	Ng1 – f3	Nb8 – c6
3	Bf1 – c4	Bf8 – c5
4	c2 – c3	Ng8 – f6
5	d2 – d4	e5 × d4
6	c3 × d4	Bc5 – b4 check
7	Nb1 – c3	d7 – d5
8	e4 × d5	Nf6 × d5
9	0-0	Bc8 – e6
10	Bc1 – g5	Bb4 – e7
11	Bc4 × Nd5	Be6 × Bd5
12	Nc3 × Bd5	Qd8 × Nd5
13	Bg5 × Be7	Nc6 × Be7
14	Rf1 – e1	f7 – f6
15	Qd1 – e2	Qd5 – d7
16	Ra1 – c1	c7 – c6
17	d4 – d5	c6 × d5
18	Nf3 – d4	Ke8 – f7
19	Nd4 – e6	Rh8 – c8
20	Qe2 – g4	g7 – g6

21 Ne6 – g5 check   Kf7 – e8

22 Re1 × Ne7 check

A lovely move! If the black king captures the rook, then the white rook at **c1** goes to **e1** check. The king is forced back to **d8** and then the knight plays to **e6** check, and when the king moves the knight moves, attacking the black queen and simultaneously leaving the black king in check from the rook.

          22 ..... Ke8 – f8

23 Re7 – f7 check   Kf8 – g8

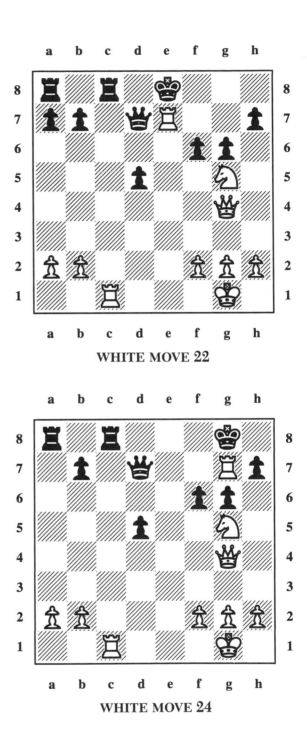

WHITE MOVE 22

24 Rf7 – g7 check

The black king cannot really take the rook. If he does, then Steinitz's queen captures the black queen with check.

          24 ..... Kg8 – h8

25 Rg7 × h7 check

Bardeleben is now in a mating net. Steinitz announces mate in ten moves.

          25 ..... Resign

Bardeleben resigns, foiling Steinitz.

WHITE MOVE 24

If the game had continued, this is what would have happened.

		25	Kh8 – g8
26	Rh7 – g7 check		Kg8 – h8
27	Qg4 – h4 check		Kh8 × Rg7

The black king can now do this as he will not lose his queen with check.

28 Qh4 – h7 check   Kg7 – f8

Bardeleben cannot take the white queen as he will be mated himself.

29 Qh7 – h8 check   Kf8 – e7
30 Qh8 – g7 check   Ke7 – e8
31 Qg7 – g8 check   Ke8 – e7
32 Qg8 – f7 check   Ke7 – d8

33 Qf7 – f8 check

This forces the black queen to block the check.

33 . . . . . Qd7 – e8

34 Ng5 – f7 check   Kd8 – d7

U.S. Chess Federation, New Windsor, NY

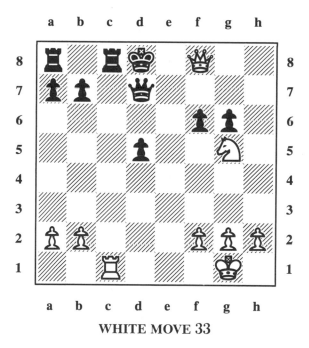

WHITE MOVE 33

35 Qf8 – d6 mate

It was a brilliant finish and it will live forever in the history of chess.

Note: Published games often use a more abbreviated notation. Throughout this book, all "move from" squares are given, and for the above game, which is not fully illustrated, "taken" pieces are identified to help you learn the game.

CHESS REVIEW

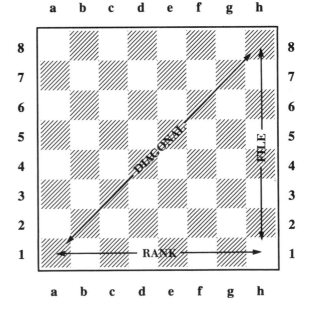

THE BOARD

Rank   Rows across board
File   Columns up and down board
Diagonal Squares corner to corner

HOW THEY MOVE

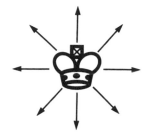

KING (K)

Moves only 1 square in any direction (on rank, file, or diagonally).

KNIGHT (N)

"Jumps" 3 squares in L shape along rank and file and "over" any man in way. Takes only on landing square.

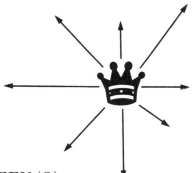

QUEEN (Q)

Moves any distance (1 to 7 squares) in any direction (on rank, file, or diagonally)

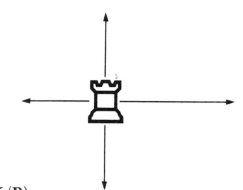

ROOK (R)

Moves any distance (1 to 7 squares) but only along rank or file.

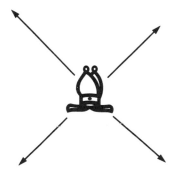

BISHOP (B)

Moves any distance (1 to 7 squares) but only diagonally.

PAWN

Moves 1 square forward only, except on first move can move forward 2 squares. Takes or captures only diagonally.

FOLLOWING CHESS MOVES

White always starts.
Dots indicate black's move.

1	(white)
1	(black)
2	(white)
2	(black)

Players move in turn. No passing.

CHESS NOTATION

—	moves to
×	takes
+	check
♯	checkmate
!	a good move
?	a bad move
0-0	short castle
0-0-0	long castle

CHESS TERMS

blocking   placing a piece in the path of an enemy checking piece to stop it from reaching the king

capturing   taking an enemy piece and standing yours in its place

castling   a special king move involving a rook jump—two moves are played as one

center of board   the four central squares— **d4, d5, e4, e5**

check   a move that attacks the king

checkmate   a check from which the king cannot escape

chessboard   a gameboard with alternating light and dark squares. It should always be placed with a white square in the near right-hand corner

diagonal   corner-to-corner direction on the chessboard

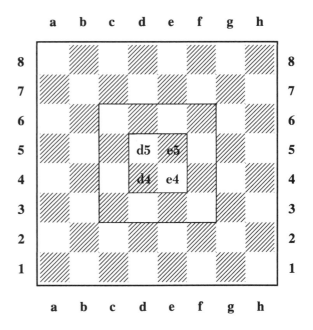

discovered check   when a piece is moved that uncovers an attack by another piece on the enemy king

draw   a game in which neither side can win

en passant   immediately capturing a pawn that has just advanced two places to alongside

endgame   finishing the game—learn to checkmate the lone king with your king and queen

files   the rows going up and down the chessboard

forced move   when a player has no choice but to make that one move

fork   an attack by one man on two enemy points

go   making a move

jump   pass over another piece. Only the knight can jump, except *See* **castling**

middle game   well into the game—use tactics like the fork and the pin

move   white moves first, then black—both constitute one chess move

open file   a file on which there are no pawns

opening   start of the game—concentrate on getting all your pieces out, one at a time

passed pawn   one that is not opposed by an enemy pawn on its way down the file

pawn   a pawn is a pawn is a pawn. They should not be referred to as pieces

perpetual check   when a king is put through a series of checks but cannot be checkmated

piece   any man except the pawn. The queen and rook are major pieces; the knight and bishop are minor pieces

pin   an attack on a piece which, if it should move, leaves a more valuable man open to capture

position   the arrangement of pieces on the board

promoting a pawn   getting a pawn through to the other side of the board where it can become a queen or any other piece

protecting   placing a second piece so that a "taking" piece would itself be in danger of capture

ranks   the rows running side-to-side across the chessboard

smothered mate   when a king is surrounded by its own pieces and unable to move out of check

touch and move   a most important rule: If you touch a piece you must move it

U.S. Chess Federation, New Windsor, NY

THIS IS TO CERTIFY
that

....

has passed the

KNIGHT'S
DRIVING TEST

Signed ....

Date ....

INDEX

JOIN THE

U.S. CHESS
FEDERATION

Congratulations on your purchase of this fine chess book from Sterling Publishing Co., Inc.! Now you can enjoy another competitive edge over other chess hobbyists by joining the more than 70,000 chessplayers who are members of the U.S. Chess Federation, the official chess organization in the U.S. since 1939.

As a U.S. Chess member, you'll receive six issues of *Chess Life* or *School Mates*, the Federation's world-famous monthly magazines. You'll also receive other benefits—discounts on chess books and equipment, the opportunity to play in official tournaments (both across the board and through the mail)—and the opportunity to obtain a national chess rating.

Say yes to U.S. Chess and we'll send you the FREE booklet "Ten Tips to Winning Chess" by International Grandmaster Arthur Bisguier.

Send to: **U.S. CHESS** FEDERATION

186 Route 9W, New Windsor, NY 12553
Attention: Dept. 91   Or call: 1-800-388-5464

☑ I'm saying yes to U.S. Chess!
Send my *free* booklet and membership card.
　　☐ Adult six-month membership $9.95 (*Chess Life**)
　　☐ Youth six-month membership $7.50 (*Chess Life**)
　　☐ Scholastic one-year membership $7.00 (*School Mates***, the bimonthly magazine for
　　　 beginners)

NAME: _____

ADDRESS: _____

CITY: _____ STATE: _____ ZIP: _____

BIRTHDATE: _____

☐ Check or money order enclosed　　☐ Bill me later
☐ American Express　☐ Discover　☐ Visa　☐ MasterCard

Exp. Date _____

(U.S. Chess is a not-for-profit membership association.
*All of your dues goes toward your *Chess Life* subscription.
**$4.50 of your $7 dues goes toward your *School Mates* subscription.)
This offer is valid only in the U.S. and is subject to expire without notice.
Membership dues are not refundable.